76 United Statesiana

76 UNITED STATESIANA

Seventy-six works of American scholarship relating to America as published during two centuries from the Revolutionary Era of the United States through the nation's Bicentennial Year

EDITED BY
EDWARD CONNERY LATHEM

Association of Research Libraries
Washington, D.C., 1976

This publication
was made possible
through a grant from
THE POWER FOUNDATION
of Ann Arbor, Michigan

INTRODUCTORY NOTE

In observance of the bicentennial of American independence this selection of books celebrates two hundred years of scholarly activity concerned with various aspects of the life and culture, the history and heritage of the United States. The seventy-six works here featured are intended to be *representative* in nature—chosen from among countless others, with focus on America or on matters American, which also might well have been singled out and cited—representative of the writings of certain of the country's principal historians, of efforts in diverse subject areas, and of different approaches and objectives in presentation. The initial seventeen date from America's first century as a nation, while the next twenty-five relate to the fifty years which immediately followed, through the time of its sesquicentennial in 1926. Twenty-nine were published during the three decades from the mid-'20s to the mid-1950s, and a final five are of the relatively recent past, 1963-76. Arrangement is chronological.

76 United Statesiana

THE
HISTORY
OF
NEW-HAMPSHIRE.

VOLUME I.

COMPREHENDING THE EVENTS OF ONE COMPLETE
CENTURY FROM THE DISCOVERY OF THE
RIVER PASCATAQUA.

By JEREMY BELKNAP, A.M.

Member of the American Philosophical Society held at Philadelphia
for promoting useful Knowledge.

Tempus edax rerum, tuque invidiosa vetustas
Omnia destruitis: vitiataque dentibus ævi
Paulatim lenta consumitis omnia morte.
Hæc perstant.   OVID.

PHILADELPHIA:
PRINTED FOR THE AUTHOR BY ROBERT AITKEN, IN
MARKET STREET, NEAR THE COFFEE-HOUSE.

M.DCC.LXXXIV.

1

In his poem "The Gift Outright," wherein he treats of the ending of this country's Colonial era, Robert Frost has written:

> Such as we were we gave ourselves outright
> (The deed of gift was many deeds of war)
> To the land vaguely realizing westward,
> But still unstoried, artless, unenhanced,
> Such as she was, such as she would become.

Throughout the American Revolution and well into the 19th Century "unstoried" the United States very largely remained, for little of a substantial nature was achieved during that interval to chronicle or interpret the new nation.

Despite the drama and significance of our separation from Great Britain and the forging of bonds of governmental union among the former provinces, and notwithstanding a development of strong nationalistic attitudes, the years of our War for Independence and its immediate aftermath saw, indeed, as much concern for annals of individual states as for telling the story of the fledgling republic itself.

Surely, no historian from that period of our early nationhood earned greater or more lasting distinction than did the Rev. Jeremy Belknap, whose *History of New Hampshire* is a landmark in American historiography—a product of scholarship important not only for its primacy and contemporary impact, but one which because of its carefully researched and dispassionate character, as well as its felicitous style, remains to this day both valuable and highly readable.

Belknap had within the realm of history a profound influence, as a result of his publications and (following his return, after a twenty-year ministry at Dover, New Hampshire, to take up a parish in his native Boston) by virtue of his central responsibility for founding the Massachusetts Historical Society, the earliest organization of its kind in the land. And it was no less a figure than William Cullen Bryant who hailed him as possessing "the high merit of being the first to make American history attractive."

Belknap's classic *History of New Hampshire* was completed in three volumes. The first was printed at Philadelphia in 1784. The second and third volumes appeared in 1791 and 1792, respectively, printed at Boston. The sustained popularity and continuing consequence of this great pioneer work are attested by the fact that reprintings of it have been brought forth in the 18th, 19th, and 20th Centuries.

MELDRIM THOMSON JR.
Governor of New Hampshire

THE AMERICAN GEOGRAPHY;

OR,

A VIEW OF THE PRESENT SITUATION

OF THE

UNITED STATES OF AMERICA.

CONTAINING

Aftronomical Geography.
Geographical Definitions.
Difcovery, and General Defcription of America.
Summary account of the Difcoveries and Settlements of North America; General View of the United, States; Of their Boundaries; Lakes; Bays and Rivers; Mountains; Productions; Population; Government; Agriculture, Commerce; Manufactures; Hiftory; Concife Account of the War, and of the important Events which have fucceeded. Biographical Sketches of feveral illuftrious Heroes.
General account of New England; Of its Boundaries; Extent; Divifions; Mountains; Rivers; Natural Hiftory; Productions; Population; Character; Trade; Hiftory.
Particular Defcriptions of the Thirteen United States, and of Kentucky, The Weftern Territory and Vermont.—Of their Extent; Civil Divifions; Chief Towns; Climates: Rivers; Mountains; Soils; Productions; Trade; Manufactures; Agriculture; Population; Character; Conftitutions; Courts of Juftice; Colleges; Academies and Schools; Religion; Iflands; Indians; Literary and Humane Societies; Springs; Curiofities; Hiftories.

Illuftrated with two Sheet Maps—One of the Southern, the other of the Northern States, neatly and elegantly engraved, and more correct than any that have hitherto been publifhed.

To which is added, a concife Abridgment of the Geography of the Britifh, Spanifh, French and Dutch Dominions in America, and the Weft Indies—Of Europe, Afia and Africa.

By JEDIDIAH MORSE.

ELIZABETH TOWN:
PRINTED BY SHEPARD KOLLOCK, FOR THE AUTHOR.
M,DCC,LXXXIX.

2

"So imperfect are all the accounts of America hitherto published, even by those who once exclusively possessed the best means of information, that from them very little knowledge of this country can be acquired. Europeans have been the sole writers of American Geography, and have too often suffered fancy to supply the place of facts, and thus have led their readers into errors, while they professed to aim at removing their ignorance. But since the United State[s] have become an independent nation, and have risen into Empire, it would be reproachful for them to suffer this ignorance to continue; and the rest of the world have a right now to expect authentic information. To furnish this has been the design of the author of the following work...." Thus wrote Jedediah Morse in the preface to the first edition of his *American Geography*.

The work of Morse, the father of American geography, represents the first attempt by an American to capture the true spirit of the nation by assessing the diversity of its landscape.

Morse, who has been described as a compiler, provides us with a detailed description of the physical character of the nation as of 1789 and how the physical character influenced the development of the nation's resources. Indeed, a great deal of effort was required to marshal the intimate detail employed in describing the individual American states.

Morse, a Congregational minister, was an enthusiastic supporter of American and Christian virtues, and these traits are ever present in his description of American geography. These and other traits, however, led Morse to be less positive in his assessment of selected qualities of individual states. For instance, his treatment of the states of the South was less positive than his treatment of New England. Such was an outgrowth of his own ethnocentrism, coupled with strong negative views regarding slavery, which he felt promoted a leisure class that lost touch with the necessity for human toil.

Views of this sort permeate much of his written work. Nevertheless, we are indebted to Morse for painstakingly providing us with a fully developed geography of the United States at a time when the new nation was, in terms of both its landscape and human character, largely unknown to the world.

HAROLD M. ROSE
President, Association of American Geographers

HISTORICAL COLLECTIONS;

CONSISTING OF

STATE PAPERS,

AND OTHER AUTHENTIC DOCUMENTS; INTENDED AS MATERIALS FOR
AN HISTORY OF THE

UNITED STATES OF AMERICA.

By EBENEZER HAZARD, A.M.
MEMBER OF THE AMERICAN PHILOSOPHICAL SOCIETY, HELD AT
PHILADELPHIA, FOR PROMOTING USEFUL KNOWLEDGE;
AND FELLOW OF THE AMERICAN ACADEMY
OF ARTS AND SCIENCES.

VOLUME I.

"Ingenium, Pietas, Artes, ac bellica Virtus,
Huc Profugæ venient, et Regna illuſtria condent,
Et Domina his Virtus erit, et Fortuna Miniſtra."

PHILADELPHIA:
Printed by T. DOBSON, for the AUTHOR.
M DCC XCII.

3

Ebenezer Hazard (1745–1817), printer and bookseller, was one of the first to appreciate that authentic documents are "the Foundation of a good American History." Accordingly, in 1774 he announced his intention to collect, transcribe, and publish the state papers of the colonies and the emerging nation. Thomas Jefferson, who understood that such a compilation would be useful to administrators, as well as indispensable to historians, co-operated warmly. So did John Adams, who judged Hazard "very capable of the Business he has undertaken—he is a Genius."

In 1778 Congress endorsed the project, recommending that the states allow Hazard to inspect their public records and furnish copies without expense. Unfortunately, Hazard's promotion to Postmaster General, which confined him to the seat of government, postponed publication until 1792.

Hazard's *Historical Collections* was the first systematic publication of documentary sources for the history of the United States. Conceiving his subject broadly, Hazard planned to include fugitive pieces, as well as official documents, and he refused to omit or alter any part of the record that might offend his readers. He was careful in transcription, assuring readers that any "errors and inaccuracies" they might see in his text were to be found in the originals. And each volume had a good index.

Urged to write a history of the United States, Hazard replied that the *Historical Collections* would "of themselves, form the best history that can be published, as they will furnish facts free from the glosses of commentators."

For want of patronage, the work was suspended after the second volume appeared in 1794. But, like all well-edited collections of documents, Hazard's for many years provided "the Foundation" for scores of histories of early America. It was in fact also the precursor of other publications by archivist-editors, among them Hezekiah Niles' *Principles and Acts of the Revolution*, Jared Sparks' *Diplomatic Correspondence of the American Revolution*, Peter Force's *American Archives*, and the *Pennsylvania Archives*, compiled by Hazard's son Samuel.

These and similar works not only made the sources of American history accessible to all, but also, in Jefferson's words, guaranteed the basic records of the nation against loss and destruction, "not by vaults and locks which fence them from the public eye and use, . . . but by such a multiplication of copies, as shall place them beyond the reach of accident."

WHITFIELD J. BELL JR.
Librarian, American Philosophical Society

HISTORY

OF THE

RISE, PROGRESS AND TERMINATION

OF THE

AMERICAN REVOLUTION.

INTERSPERSED WITH

Biographical, Political and Moral Observations.

IN THREE VOLUMES.

BY MRS. MERCY WARREN,
OF PLYMOUTH, (MASS.)

..........Troubled on every side..............
perplexed, but not in despair; persecuted, but not forsaken;
cast down, but not destroyed. *ST. PAUL.*

O God! thy arm was here.........
And not to us, but to thy arm alone,
Ascribe we all. *SHAKESPEARE.*

VOL. I.

BOSTON:
PRINTED BY MANNING AND LORING,
For E. LARKIN, No. 47, CORNHILL.
1805.

4

In "An Address to the Inhabitants of the United States of America" Mercy Otis Warren, prefacing her three-volume *History of the Rise, Progress and Termination of the American Revolution*, explained: "At a period when every manly arm was occupied, and every trait of talent or activity engaged, either in the cabinet or the field, apprehensive, that amidst the sudden convulsions, crowded scenes, and rapid changes, that flowed in quick succession, many circumstances might escape the more busy and active members of society, I have been induced to improve the leisure Providence had lent, to record as they passed, in the following pages, the new and unexperienced events exhibited in a land previously blessed with peace, liberty, simplicity, and virtue."

Mercy Warren set down the history of the Revolution as she had observed it. More than an observer, she was in the center of the action. Sister of lawyer-politician James Otis Jr., close friend of John Adams, and wife of James Warren (merchant, farmer, and legislator), Mercy had not only listened and recorded, but encouraged and advised. She did so while devoting attention to her five sons and suffering through family tragedies and the effect of her own anxieties.

Torn between an urge to be actively engaged in the Revolution and a fear that such activity was unbecoming to a virtuous female, Mercy Warren was encouraged by John and Abigail Adams to lend her talents to the cause of liberty, and the *Boston Gazette* published her satires ridiculing Thomas Hutchinson and the Tories.

Again with John Adams' urging, she was a recorder of events from her unique position of proximity to all the main participants. It is difficult to know now how many of her views on the characters of John Hancock, Hutchinson, and other leaders in the struggle were those of her husband and John Adams, of Sam Adams and the Otises, and how much her opinions influenced them. That she had a strong influence is well documented.

The three-volume *History* has been regarded as a source book for the republican view, as well as a record of the disagreements within the Whig party. Sam Adams' and Mercy Warren's strong Puritan desire for a truly representative government had to be modified by John Adams and others to get agreement for the Constitution and the formation of the new country. This resulted in a breach in the close friendship of John Adams and Mrs. Warren, but even so important a difference did not deter Mercy Warren from her writing.

VIRGINIA P. WHITNEY
University Librarian, Rutgers University

AMERICAN ORNITHOLOGY;

OR,

THE NATURAL HISTORY

OF THE

BIRDS OF THE UNITED STATES:

ILLUSTRATED WITH PLATES

Engraved and Colored from Original drawings taken from Nature.

BY ALEXANDER WILSON.

VOL. I.

PHILADELPHIA:

PUBLISHED BY BRADFORD AND INSKEEP.

PRINTED BY ROBERT CARR.

1808.

5 Few early works of natural history are more thoroughly American than Wilson's *American Ornithology*. Discussing the book in *The Medical Repository* (1811), Samuel Mitchill observed, "... it ought to be constantly borne in mind that the exquisite paper, the distinct type, the correct engraving, and the fine colouring are all domestic; and the same American character belongs to the press-work, the binding, and the other mechanical parts of the work...." But the significance of Wilson's great work goes far beyond its physical qualities.

The book antedates Audubon by several years and is the first American color-plate bird book published in America. It is exceptional in its scope, its accuracy, and its completeness. Three hundred and twenty figures of birds are included, representing two hundred and sixty-two species.

Wilson covered only the eastern United States north of Florida, but during the next hundred years only twenty-three indigenous land birds have been added to Wilson's list. Twenty-three specimens originally described by Wilson still retain their validity in the latest *Checklist* of the American Ornithologists Union.

Wilson's work is inevitably compared with Audubon's, and the pat judgment is that Audubon was a great artist with a talent for ornithology, while Wilson was a great ornithologist with artistic talent. No one claims that Wilson is Audubon's equal as an artist, yet Wilson's direct approach to bird portraiture, and the freshness and naturalness he imparts to his subjects, have strongly influenced contemporary bird painters, such as Roger Tory Peterson, whose *Field Guide to the Birds* has revolutionized field ornithology and has made every bird watcher an expert. Thus, Wilson more than Audubon deserves to share credit for the phenomenal popularity that "birding" now enjoys.

More important, Wilson's work promoted the cause of natural history and helped to prepare the way for the conservation movement and present-day concern for the environment.

The first volume of *American Ornithology* appeared in September 1808. The eighth was in the press when Wilson died in August of 1813 (both this volume and the ninth were edited by George Ord and issued in 1814). The set is of imperial-quarto size, with seventy-six color plates distributed nearly uniformly throughout. From Wilson's original watercolors the plates were engraved on copper, principally by Lawson and Warnicke, hand-colored by Alexander Rider and others, bound with the text, and issued by Bradford and Innskeep of Philadelphia.

JOHN P. MCDONALD
Director of University Libraries, University of Connecticut

THE
HISTORY OF PRINTING
IN
AMERICA.
WITH A
BIOGRAPHY OF PRINTERS,
AND AN
ACCOUNT OF NEWSPAPERS.
TO WHICH IS PREFIXED A CONCISE VIEW OF
THE DISCOVERY AND PROGRESS OF THE ART
IN
OTHER PARTS OF THE WORLD.

IN TWO VOLUMES.

BY ISAIAH THOMAS,
PRINTER, WORCESTER, MASSACHUSETTS.

Volume I.

PRINTING dispels the gloom of mental night—
Hail! pleasing fountain of all cheering light!
How like the radiant orb which gives the day,
And o'er the earth sends forth th' enlight'ning ray!

WORCESTER:
FROM THE PRESS OF ISAIAH THOMAS, JUN.
ISAAC STURTEVANT, PRINTER.
1810.

6 "Isaiah Thomas a poor child" was bound as an apprentice to an "ignorant printer" when he was but six years old. He stood at the case setting type before he could read or write, and the printing office was the only school he ever had. However, his enterprise was such that by the time he was eleven years old the responsibility for running his indolent master's shop was largely his.

Born in Boston in 1749, Isaiah Thomas grew to manhood in turbulent times, at the very center of revolutionary ferment. In 1770 he began publishing the *Massachusetts Spy*, a newspaper made famous by its support of the people's liberty. The inevitable ensuing conflict with the royal government strengthened Thomas's dedicated patriotism. When the British occupied Boston in 1775, he joined Paul Revere in alarming the countryside and as a minuteman fought at Lexington and Concord.

In the new nation he rose to become the leading printer-publisher of his generation, employing over one hundred and fifty people in printing offices, bindery, paper mill, and bookstores. When he retired in 1802, a wealthy man, he devoted himself to book collecting, scholarship, and writing *The History of Printing in America*.

First published in 1810 in two volumes, this work remains a primary source for any investigation of printing and publishing in North America. The beginnings of printing on the continent are documented, with sections on papermaking, typefounding, engraving, and printing presses. The printers and their works in each of the states and territories, as well as the Canadian provinces, are treated in great detail. The volumes contain material which is available nowhere else, and they are still the recognized authority on the subject.

A second, revised edition was published in 1874, and in 1970 that edition was republished as a single volume in amended form, and more recently it has been issued in paperback.

Isaiah Thomas's library, his voluminous correspondence, and personal papers which were source materials for the *History* later became the cornerstone collection of the American Antiquarian Society, which he founded and served as first president. Full of honors and years, he died in 1831.

RODERICK D. STINEHOUR
Printer; President, The Stinehour Press

COMMENTARIES

ON

AMERICAN LAW.

BY JAMES KENT.

VOLUME I.

NEW-YORK:
PUBLISHED BY O. HALSTED.
Law Buildings, Nassau-street.

1826.

7

The *Commentaries on American Law* by James Kent (1763–1847), which were first published from 1826 through 1830, have been called "the most important American law book of the nineteenth century." Patterned after Blackstone, they dealt systematically with the entire corpus of American jurisprudence and provided basic instruction for generations of American lawyers and others interested in government and jurisprudence.

The *Commentaries* were immediately and immensely popular. Five editions were published during Kent's lifetime and nine thereafter. Oliver Wendell Holmes Jr. was the editor of the twelfth edition, which appeared in 1847.

As a young practitioner, Kent had been closely associated with the Federalist party of Alexander Hamilton and John Jay, and through their influence had obtained a professorship at Columbia in 1793. He served only briefly, however, as he did not find the lecturing congenial, nor did his lectures attract many students.

In 1798, when Jay was governor of New York, Kent was named to its supreme court. In six years he became its chief justice and then, in 1814, chancellor of New York. He held that office until 1823, when he reached the mandatory retirement age of sixty.

Within four months, Kent was reappointed to Columbia and for three terms—in 1824, 1825, and 1826—he delivered the lectures which formed the background for the *Commentaries*. Again, however, he found teaching no easy task and, "having got heartily tired of lecturing," he abandoned it in 1826. Thereafter, though still nominally a professor, Kent devoted his remaining life to the *Commentaries*.

Kent's years on the bench, marked as they were by great distinction, enabled him in his *Commentaries* to go beyond Blackstone. In the first place, Kent reflected the changes that had taken place in the world and the law since 1765. Secondly, his knowledge of the law was, of necessity, more precise than that of the less-experienced Blackstone. Finally, his *Commentaries* dealt with American Law, not the law of England, except to the extent of its relevance.

Together with the *Commentaries on the Constitution of the United States* by his friend Joseph Story (1779–1845), who was a justice of the Supreme Court of the United States and a professor of law at Harvard, Kent's *Commentaries* served as a standard reference work for American lawyers and judges for many years.

JUSTIN A. STANLEY
President, American Bar Association

AMERICAN

MEDICAL BIOGRAPHY:

OR

MEMOIRS OF EMINENT PHYSICIANS

WHO HAVE

Flourished in America.

TO WHICH IS PREFIXED

A

SUCCINCT HISTORY

OF

MEDICAL SCIENCE IN THE UNITED STATES,

FROM THE

FIRST SETTLEMENT OF THE COUNTRY.

BY JAMES THACHER, M.D.

Fellow of the American Academy of Arts and Sciences; Honorary Member of the New-York Historical Society, and of the New-York Horticultural Society, &c.; Author of the American New Dispensatory, of the Modern Practice of Physic, and of the Military Journal.

TWO VOLUMES IN ONE.

VOL. I.

" Thou shalt lie down
With patriarchs of the infant world—with kings,
The powerful of the earth—the wise, the good,
Fair forms, and hoary seers of ages past,
All in one mighty sepulchre." BRYANT.

BOSTON:
RICHARDSON & LORD AND COTTONS & BARNARD.

1828.

8

James Thacher (1754–1844) stands foremost among the chroniclers of medicine in Colonial America and of the physicians who practiced it. His *American Medical Biography*, published in 1828, has remained a classic of medical history for almost a century and a half. The book, published as two volumes in one, is composed of one hundred and sixty-three biographies on seven hundred and sixteen octavo pages. Opening with an engaging history of early American medicine, the biographies include fourteen lively portraits of eminent physicians of the time. Among these are Benjamin Rush of Philadelphia, distinguished physician and patriot who signed the Declaration of Independence, and John C. Warren of Boston, the renowned surgeon who pioneered in the use of ether as the first effective surgical anesthetic.

American Medical Biography is significant for two other reasons, however. First, it is a fount of information from which the reader may envision Colonial medicine at its most typical. Physicians of the period, for example, included physic, surgery, and midwifery in their practices. Medical specialization was virtually unknown prior to 1800, except on limited terms.

And second, the volume recounts the lives of somewhat more ordinary, as well as extraordinary, physicians, thus preserving a wealth of biographical information that otherwise would have been lost.

This wealth includes evidence of timeless clinical acumen, and—happily for the reader—of equally timeless human eccentricity. Of the former, our biographer says that Dr. Pardon Bowen of Providence, Rhode Island, was fully aware that disease often has both emotional and physiological causes, a fact which even today's space-age physician can forget.

And of the latter, meet Seth Bird of Litchfield, Connecticut, who not only had his own coffin built to his specifications, but kept it in his office, to the discomfort of patients and visitors alike. Dr. Bird was wont to tell friends that he "would slide into it in a few days."

Fortunately for posterity, physician and biographer James Thacher did not "slide into" his coffin until May 24, 1844, in his ninety-first year. Born at Barnstable, on Cape Cod, his own medical career included extensive service as a military surgeon, and, subsequently, forty years of skilled surgical practice in Plymouth, Massachusetts, where he lived with his wife, Susannah Hayward Thacher.

It is as the author of *American Medical Biography*, however, that the name of James Thacher endures to this day.

RICHARD E. PALMER
President, American Medical Association

AN AMERICAN DICTIONARY

OF THE

ENGLISH LANGUAGE:

INTENDED TO EXHIBIT,

I. The origin, affinities and primary signification of English words, as far as they have been ascertained.
II. The genuine orthography and pronunciation of words, according to general usage, or to just principles of analogy.
III. Accurate and discriminating definitions, with numerous authorities and illustrations.

TO WHICH ARE PREFIXED,

AN INTRODUCTORY DISSERTATION

ON THE

ORIGIN, HISTORY AND CONNECTION OF THE

LANGUAGES OF WESTERN ASIA AND OF EUROPE,

AND A CONCISE GRAMMAR

OF THE

ENGLISH LANGUAGE.

BY NOAH WEBSTER, LL. D.

IN TWO VOLUMES.

VOL. I.

He that wishes to be counted among the benefactors of posterity, must add, by his own toil, to the acquisitions of his ancestors.—*Rambler.*

NEW YORK:
PUBLISHED BY S. CONVERSE.

PRINTED BY HEZEKIAH HOWE—NEW HAVEN.

1828.

9 *An American Dictionary of the English Language* by Noah Webster was published in 1828, when its compiler was seventy years of age. It represented twenty-five years of intense labor and served as the testament of a man who believed that language was a reflection of distinct environmental boundaries and national attitudes.

Webster's spelling book, which sold sixty million copies between 1783 and 1890, included some new American words, as well as changes in English spelling: "honor" for "honour" and "plow" for "plough." The *Dictionary* continued this practice by including words used in common American speech. And words like "congress" and "assembly" were redefined to conform to American interpretations.

Some seventy thousand words—fifteen thousand more than any previous English lexicon—were listed and defined. Although only twenty-five hundred copies of the first edition were printed, the work established Webster as a lexicographer of international repute.

The *Dictionary* was dedicated to his "fellow citizens, not with frigid indifference, but with my ardent wishes for their improvement and their happiness; and for the continued increase of the wealth, the learning, the moral and religious elevation of character, and the glory of my country."

Born on a farm in West Hartford, Connecticut, in 1758, Webster was graduated from Yale College in 1778 and was admitted to the bar in 1781. He died in New Haven, May 28, 1843, at age eighty-five. He was largely responsible for our first copyright laws and served in the legislatures of both Connecticut and Massachusetts, but it is as a schoolmaster and lexicographer that he is best remembered.

RUTHERFORD D. ROGERS
University Librarian, Yale University

A

HISTORY

OF THE

UNITED STATES,

FROM THE DISCOVERY OF THE AMERICAN CONTINENT
TO THE PRESENT TIME.

BY GEORGE BANCROFT.

VOL. I.

BOSTON:
PUBLISHED BY CHARLES BOWEN.
LONDON:
R. J. KENNETT.
......
1834.

10

The publication in 1834 of the first volume of George Bancroft's multi-volume *History of the United States* proved to be more than a literary event. It was an eloquent testimonial to the national purpose. First of the native historians to undertake a large-scale history of the American nation, Bancroft, despite his avowed patriotism, was no chauvinist but a true cosmopolite. Harvard-educated, with a brief career as a clergyman and teacher, he spent two years abroad, mostly at Göttingen, before setting out to write his monumental work. Later, as America's envoy to the Court of St. James's and as minister to Berlin, he enlarged his linguistic facilities, enriched his European intellectual contacts, and acquired a preference for what he deemed to be the Anglo-Saxon and German traditions of freedom.

A democrat with a small and capital "d," Bancroft combined the arduous effort of producing a ten-volume history of the United States with an active career in politics. Collector of the port of Boston under President Van Buren and a cabinet officer in the Polk administration, Bancroft informed his "history" with both his democratic convictions and his intense nationalism.

"It is a noble matter, and I am heartily glad to have it nobly treated," Ralph Waldo Emerson commented when the first volume of the *History* appeared. Emerson's views were endorsed by innumerable fellow Americans, who kept buying Bancroft's books—until by 1875 the *History* had gone through twenty-five editions.

For the centenary of the nation, Bancroft brought out a revised edition of his *History* in six volumes, to which six years later he added his two-volume *History of the Formation of the Constitution of the United States*. Between 1883 and 1885 "The Author's Last Revision" of the monumental work came off the press. Thus, at the advanced age of eighty-five, Bancroft had triumphantly completed a magnum opus begun some sixty years before.

Time has not been too gentle to Bancroft's *History*. Its ornamental prose style, demanded of historians who lived in an age when history was a branch of belles lettres, is less congenial to a more skeptical time. A prodigious digger and copier of pertinent manuscript sources abroad, Bancroft used his sources unsystematically. No historian since his day has, however, managed to command so large a readership, nor have any of Bancroft's successors surpassed him in his ability to evoke that sense of mission and dedication to freedom which the author felt especially distinguished America's role in history.

RICHARD B. MORRIS
President, American Historical Association

HISTORY

OF THE

RISE AND PROGRESS

OF THE

ARTS OF DESIGN

IN THE UNITED STATES.

BY WILLIAM DUNLAP,
Vice President of the National Academy of Design, Author of the History of the
American Theatre,—Biography of G. F. Cooke,—&c.

IN TWO VOLUMES.
VOL. I.

NEW-YORK:
GEORGE P. SCOTT AND CO. PRINTERS, 33 ANN STREET.
1834.

11

In the early years of the republic, American artists had difficulty establishing their place in society or even maintaining for themselves a sense of their own destiny. Although they joined their political compatriots in judging their activity as fundamental to a flourishing posterity, it was some while before their confidence in the future could make them happy with the present and respectful of their past. In 1834 art and its artists were confirmed as a part of the fabric of American culture by a remarkable pair of volumes produced by an equally remarkable man, William Dunlap. *History of the Rise and Progress of the Arts of Design in the United States* was a gathering together of the past and the present, to serve American art as a solid foundation for the future.

William Dunlap was born in 1766, studied painting in England under Benjamin West, became an active playwright and producer in the theatre (he published a *History of the American Theatre* in 1832), and was a persistent joiner and promoter of artist organizations. By the time he began to solicit information from his artist friends to construct his monumental work, he had lived through several careers. He was, quite literally, a major element in the histories he was compiling.

Although called the "American Vasari," he was rather more modest than that self-conscious Tuscan, and made less of an effort to bend history to a controllable shape. Yet, his histories are not just chronicles of events and accumulations of biographies, but testimonies of faith. Dunlap believed in the importance of the arts —all of the arts—in a democracy, and he set out to show that they had developed and would flourish, even against odds. Thus he attempted to allay the self-doubt of artists to come, and succeeded in setting a pattern for thinking about art in American society that would last for a very long time.

History of the Rise and Progress of the Arts of Design in the United States was published in New York in 1834. Frank W. Bayley and Charles E. Goodspeed prepared a revised edition in three volumes (Boston, 1918), and there have been later publications. Although succeeded by histories that were more chastely objective and formulated according to more sophisticated methods, Dunlap's work has remained the fount from which most studies of early American art must spring.

JOSHUA C. TAYLOR
Director, National Collection of Fine Arts

A

MANUAL OF THE

BOTANY

OF THE

NORTHERN UNITED STATES,

FROM NEW ENGLAND TO WISCONSIN AND SOUTH TO OHIO
AND PENNSYLVANIA INCLUSIVE,

(THE MOSSES AND LIVERWORTS BY WM. S. SULLIVANT,)

ARRANGED

ACCORDING TO THE NATURAL SYSTEM;

WITH AN INTRODUCTION, CONTAINING A REDUCTION OF THE GENERA
TO THE LINNÆAN ARTIFICIAL CLASSES AND ORDERS,
OUTLINES OF THE ELEMENTS OF BOTANY,
A GLOSSARY, ETC.

BY ASA GRAY, M. D.,
FISHER PROFESSOR OF NATURAL HISTORY IN HARVARD UNIVERSITY.

BOSTON & CAMBRIDGE:
JAMES MUNROE AND COMPANY.
LONDON: JOHN CHAPMAN.
1848.

12

Asa Gray (1810–1888), of Scotch-Irish ancestry, a native of Paris, New York, was educated as a physician but spent his entire life as a botanist. Outstandingly gifted as scientist, teacher, and writer, Gray's greatest achievement was his elaboration of the descriptive botany of North America. His writings comprise over three hundred and fifty books, monographs, and shorter papers on this vast subject.

American expansion westward and overseas during Gray's lifetime produced a flood of botanical returns. A program of plant classification on a continental scale was needed. To this end Gray and an early teacher and associate, John Torrey, commenced preparation of a magnum opus, *Flora of North America*, the first volume of which appeared in 1838.

Gray wrote his *Manual of the Botany of the Northern United States* to fill a need that the slower-moving *Flora* could not fill. Probably Gray's most important work, the *Manual* appeared in 1848 and went through five editions during Gray's lifetime, and more by his Harvard successors. It remains an indispensable book for the student of American botany.

Fortunate the scientist gifted with Gray's talent for the written word! Of one of his writings a reviewer commented, "The botanist is yet to be born who could write a more clear, accurate, and compact account of the flora of any country."

In 1864, Gray presented the Gray Herbarium to Harvard University. The herbarium contained over two hundred thousand specimens and a library of two thousand volumes. By the time of his death it had doubled in size.

Gray was one of the founders of the National Academy of Sciences (1873), president of the American Academy of Arts and Sciences (1863–73), president of the American Association for the Advancement of Science (1872), and a regent of the Smithsonian Institution (1874–88). His writings, now available primarily in the research libraries of the country, record a bright chapter in American scientific achievement.

PHILIP HANDLER
President, National Academy of Sciences

HISTORY

OF THE

CONSPIRACY OF PONTIAC,

AND THE WAR OF THE

NORTH AMERICAN TRIBES

AGAINST THE

ENGLISH COLONIES

AFTER THE

CONQUEST OF CANADA.

By FRANCIS PARKMAN, Jr.

"Deesse nobis terra, in quâ vivamus; in quâ moriamur, non potest."
Tacit. Ann. xiii. 56.

BOSTON:
CHARLES C. LITTLE AND JAMES BROWN.
LONDON: RICHARD BENTLEY.
1851.

13 At an early age Francis Parkman was enamoured of forest life and Indians. As a Harvard freshman a vacation trip to the Magalloway and Lake George led to his determination to write the story of the "Old French War," and he enlisted the help of Jared Sparks in discovering "authorities sufficiently minute to satisfy me." While attending law school, under family pressure, Parkman continued his studies in Indian history and ethnology. He outlined his major undertaking in a letter to Martin Brimmer, "I now resolved to write the history of the Indian War under Pontiac, as offering peculiar opportunities for exhibiting forest life and Indian character; and to this end I began to collect materials by travel and correspondence."

Visits to the West in 1845 and 1846 were in the interest of his health, as well as giving him personal knowledge of Indian life and the topography of the area. Failing eyesight forced Parkman to depend on friends to read to him the extensive files of documents and letters as he undertook the writing of his first historical work.

Without the use of sight, he had to resort to a gridiron or frame of parallel wires, laid on the page, to guide the hand. Despite being able to write only three or four lines a day at the outset, he completed the book in about three years.

The preface to the *History of the Conspiracy of Pontiac* (1851) notes that the conquest of Canada was an event of momentous consequence in American history and indicates that the object of this work is "to portray the American forest and the American Indian at the period when both received their final doom." The work begins with an introductory discussion of the Indian tribes east of the Mississippi, followed by the role of France and England in the new world, their collision, conflict with the Indians, the Indian successes on the Western frontier, the Eastern backlash, and the final events leading to the assassination of Pontiac.

The Conspiracy of Pontiac outlines the main thrust of Parkman's writings, a series of outstanding volumes on "France and England in North America." A new enlarged edition, published in 1870, incorporates new material found in the British Museum. Enjoying continued popularity, this work, rightly considered a classic, has gone through many editions and reprintings, including a paperback edition of 1962 containing a new introduction by Samuel Eliot Morison.

Dr. John Fiske, in a memorial tribute, summed up the role of Parkman: "He was a great historian because coupled with his knowledge were a philosophic insight and a poetic instinct.... Parkman is the most American of all our historians because he deals with purely American history...."

PHILIP J. MCNIFF
Director, Boston Public Library

HISTORICAL

AND

STATISTICAL INFORMATION,

RESPECTING THE

HISTORY, CONDITION AND PROSPECTS

OF THE

INDIAN TRIBES OF THE UNITED STATES:

COLLECTED AND PREPARED UNDER THE DIRECTION

OF THE

BUREAU OF INDIAN AFFAIRS,

PER ACT OF CONGRESS OF MARCH 3D, 1847,

BY HENRY R. SCHOOLCRAFT, LL. D.

ILLUSTRATED BY S. EASTMAN, CAPT. U. S. A.

Published by Authority of Congress.

PART I.

PHILADELPHIA:
LIPPINCOTT, GRAMBO & COMPANY,
(SUCCESSORS TO GRIGG, ELLIOT & CO.)
1851.

14 As an enterprising young man of twenty-four, Henry Rowe Schoolcraft undertook a mineralogical exploration of the Indian country of southern Missouri and Arkansas in 1817–18. Publication of his report on the lead mines of Missouri gave him a reputation as a geologist and won him an invitation to join the Lewis Cass exploratory expedition to the upper Mississippi and the copper country of Lake Superior. His experience with the Indians of northern Michigan, gained on this expedition, led to Schoolcraft's appointment in 1822 as Indian agent for the Lake Superior region and as superintendent of Indian affairs for all of Michigan from 1836 to 1841.

A growing national interest in the American Indian during the mid-century decades was reflected in the publication of a number of highly important works. George Catlin issued his handsomely illustrated *Letters and Notes on the Manners, Customs, and Condition of the North American Indians* in 1841. Lewis Henry Morgan's *League of the Ho-dé-no-sau-nee, or Iroquois* appeared in 1851.

Schoolcraft authored several works during the period, including a statistical study of the Iroquois undertaken at the request of the New York legislature, and followed by the more popular *Notes on the Iroquois* in 1847. His investigation preparatory to writing the latter work brought home to him the dearth of reliable information about the American Indian and reinforced his conviction that they were a much misunderstood people who were being unjustly treated under public policy. As a consequence, Schoolcraft undertook, with the aid of a group of supporters, to persuade Congress to this point of view and was instrumental in securing the passage of legislation authorizing the Secretary of War to collect and digest "a census and statistics of the various Indian tribes, and such material as will tend to illustrate their history, present conditions and future prospects."

Schoolcraft himself was employed to perform this task, and the result of his labors appeared in six large quarto volumes between 1851 and 1857, entitled *Historical and Statistical Information, Respecting the History, Condition and Prospects of the Indian Tribes of the United States.*

In assembling his material Schoolcraft had to rely on the experience of many others, since his compendium covered all categories of knowledge concerning the Indian tribes. In no subject area was his treatment exhaustive; nevertheless the work remains as a monument in the history of ethnological study in America and an invaluable addition to Indian archaeology and history.

FREDERICK H. WAGMAN
Director, University of Michigan Library

CONTRIBUTIONS

TO

THE NATURAL HISTORY

OF THE

UNITED STATES OF AMERICA.

BY

LOUIS AGASSIZ.

FIRST MONOGRAPH.

IN THREE PARTS. — I. ESSAY ON CLASSIFICATION. — II. NORTH AMERICAN TESTUDINATA. —
III. EMBRYOLOGY OF THE TURTLE; WITH THIRTY-FOUR PLATES.

VOL. I.

BOSTON:
LITTLE, BROWN AND COMPANY.
LONDON: TRÜBNER & CO.
1857.

15

If his most significant scientific achievements were produced in Europe, it was in America as a lecturer, teacher, and leader that the Swiss-American Jean Louis Rodolphe Agassiz made his greatest contribution to natural science. During his student years at Munich and his fourteen years with the faculty at Neuchâtel he published his monumental volumes on fossil fishes, on fresh-water fish forms, and on the theory and significance of glaciation. But it was in America, during the last twenty-five years of his life, that Agassiz developed his view of the role natural history should play in science, in education, in life.

Agassiz came to the United States at the height of an already brilliant career in Europe, to hold a chair in natural history at Harvard from 1848 until his death in 1873. The idea for *Contributions to the Natural History of the United States* shaped itself after he had been at Harvard for some years. Colossal in concept, *Contributions* was conceived as a ten-volume epic, each part on a different subject and complete in itself.

Four volumes only of the finely illustrated *Contributions* were completed between 1857 and 1862. Thereafter, ill health and other pressures prevented further work on the project.

Included in the four completed monographs, the last major contributions by Agassiz to biological science, were three highly technical works (on the embryology of American turtles and on the Radiata) and the *Essay on Classification*, published as Part I. The *Essay* was the volume of greatest popular interest, setting forth Agassiz' fundamental views of the natural world as he perceived it. Considered his most significant and revealing contribution to philosophy and synthesis in his field, the *Essay* reflects Agassiz' steadfast oppositon to Darwinism, revealing clearly his conviction that diversity and similarity of structure in the animal world were the expression of a divine plan, rather than evidence of common origin.

Agassiz' popularity and influence as a teacher and a lecturer spread through all walks of life. More than any one person, he shaped the future of America's naturalists in many ways. And he left a trail of great natural history institutions behind him to serve as a lasting monument: the Museum of Comparative Zoology at Harvard and the Marine Biological Laboratory at Woods Hole, which he founded or organized; the American Museum of Natural History in New York, founded by his student Bickmore; and the National Museum of Natural History of the Smithsonian Institution, whose scientific course he influenced immensely.

THOMAS D. NICHOLSON
Director, American Museum of Natural History

A

DICTIONARY

OF

Books relating to America,

FROM ITS DISCOVERY TO THE PRESENT TIME.

By JOSEPH SABIN.

Volume I.

"A painfull work it is I'll assure you, and more than difficult, wherein what toyle hath been taken, as no man thinketh so no man believeth, but he hath made the triall."
Ant. à Wood, Preface to the History of Oxford.

New-York:
JOSEPH SABIN, 84 NASSAU STREET.
1868.

16

Joseph Sabin's *Dictionary* represents the most ambitious single-handed project ever attempted by a bibliographer. The compiler was thirty-five in 1856 when he conceived of recording every known book about the Americas. He seemed well aware of the task before him when he quoted Anthony Wood, the 17th Century historian of Oxford, on the title page of the first published volume: "A painfull work it is I'll assure you, and more than difficult, wherein what toyle hath been taken, as no man thinketh so no man believeth, but he hath made the triall."

As an American bookseller in the 1840s and 1850s, Sabin had made thirty trips to Europe to attend major sales and search for rare books. He became, also, an auctioneer who catalogued scores of libraries and conducted sales where record prices were often set (eight thousand dollars in 1881 for Brinley's Gutenberg Bible). He published two distinguished series of reprints of early Americana that stimulated collecting and provided scholars with facsimiles of rare volumes. Such were the various pursuits of the man now remembered as America's pre-eminent bibliographer.

Sabin understood the need for his great work. It is a tribute to his competence and dedication that before his death in 1881 he was able to reach the letter "N" in his *Dictionary* and complete over fifty-eight thousand detailed entries. He had issued a prospectus for the work in December 1866, and the first four parts of the first volume appeared the following year. After his death the project was continued by Wilberforce Eames, and it was completed in 1936 by a team headed by R. W. G. Vail.

The final work runs to twenty-nine volumes and includes over one hundred and six thousand entries (most of which provide collations, locations of copies, and in many instances annotations fixing the historical context of the item). The total number of editions recorded in the *Dictionary* has been estimated at more than double the number of entries.

Conceived over a century ago and requiring ninety years to complete, *A Dictionary of Books Relating to America, from Its Discovery to the Present Time*, which the compiler caption-titled *Bibliotheca Americana* and we now refer to simply as "Sabin," remains the most indispensable bibliographical tool in the field of American studies.

KENNETH NEBENZAHL
Rare Books Dealer;
President, Kenneth Nebenzahl Incorporated

THE FIRST CENTURY

OF

THE REPUBLIC:

A REVIEW OF AMERICAN PROGRESS.

BY

The Rev. THEODORE D. WOOLSEY, D.D., LL.D.; F. A. P. BARNARD, LL.D.; Hon. DAVID A. WELLS; Hon. FRANCIS A. WALKER; Prof. T. STERRY HUNT; Prof. WILLIAM G. SUMNER; EDWARD ATKINSON; Prof. THEODORE GILL; EDWIN P. WHIPPLE; Prof. W. H. BREWER; EUGENE LAWRENCE; The Rev. JOHN F. HURST, D.D.; BENJAMIN VAUGHAN ABBOTT; AUSTIN A. FLINT, M.D.; S. S. CONANT; EDWARD H. KNIGHT; AND CHARLES L. BRACE.

NEW YORK:

HARPER & BROTHERS, PUBLISHERS,

FRANKLIN SQUARE.

1876.

17

The population of the country was forty-six million, the federal union consisted of thirty-eight states (Colorado had been admitted on August first), and Ulysses S. Grant was the occupant of the White House when, in 1876, the United States marked the centennial year of its independence. Just as now, during our bicentennial year, the celebration of that historic milestone included many public events, the featured one being the vast exposition held at Philadelphia.

The anniversary also called forth various observances in print, among them *The First Century of the Republic*. This single volume accomplished within its five hundred pages a comprehensive review of the country since the time of its founding, focusing on social, economic, industrial, and cultural progress.

Conceived as a supplement to the Centennial Exposition, which featured the newest triumphs of technology, the book, by its own description, "connects the present with the past, showing the beginnings of great enterprises, tracing through consecutive states their development, and associating with them the individual thought and labor by which they have been brought to perfection."

This work, most of which had been published in *Harper's Magazine*, has no single author. Rather, it is a compilation of seventeen essays by leading authorities —men like President Emeritus Woolsey of Yale, President Barnard of Columbia, the noted economist David Wells, and geologist T. Sterry Hunt. Each individual, working wholly independently, gave to the volume the benefit of his own particular and eminent expertise.

The imposing qualifications of its authors did not, however, hinder the popular appeal of the book; it was designed not only to celebrate America's history but, also, to teach it.

As we now stand at the end of our country's second century, we are indeed fortunate to have at hand a prime example of how we viewed our progress at the end of her first century.

EDWARD W. BROOKE
United States Senator from Massachusetts;
Chairman, American Revolution Bicentennial Board

A HISTORY

OF THE

PEOPLE OF THE UNITED STATES,

FROM THE REVOLUTION TO THE CIVIL WAR.

BY
JOHN BACH McMASTER.

IN FIVE VOLUMES.
VOLUME I.

NEW YORK:
D. APPLETON AND COMPANY,
1, 3, AND 5 BOND STREET.
1883.

18

The publication in 1883 of the first volume of John Bach McMaster's *A History of the People of the United States* signaled a significant new departure in the writing of American history. While other historians were writing with the conventional emphasis on war and politics, McMaster instantly engaged the attention and interest of his readers with this opening declaration: "The subject of my narrative is the history of people of the United States."

He went on to say that although much needed to be written about wars, Presidents, Congresses, and treaties, the people would be his chief theme. He would describe the dress, the occupations, the amusements, the changes of manners and morals, the rise and progress of mechanical inventions and discoveries, and how free education and a free press had disseminated knowledge and advanced the arts and sciences.

Drawing heavily on newspapers, magazines, and other contemporary sources, he fulfilled his commitment to mingle social, economic, and political history. The first volume was an immediate success and established McMaster as the founder of the modern school of social history in the United States.

That initial volume was followed during the next thirty years by seven additional volumes, the last of which was published in 1913. In all, seventeen volumes and some twenty articles constitute the contributions of John Bach McMaster, before his death in 1932, to American history.

McMaster's origins may help explain his approach to history. Born in Brooklyn in 1852, he attended public schools in New York and was graduated from City College with an engineering degree in 1877. He then became an instructor in civil engineering in Princeton, but his keen interest in history prevailed, and upon publication of the first volume of his *History* in 1883, he accepted a chair in American history at the University of Pennsylvania, where he remained for thirty-seven years until his retirement in 1922.

Through his publications and his advanced students and through his textbooks—more than two and a half million copies of which were sold during his lifetime—McMaster exerted a profound and lasting influence on the study and writing of American history.

RICHARD DE GENNARO
Director of Libraries, University of Pennsylvania

Aboriginal America

NARRATIVE AND CRITICAL

HISTORY OF AMERICA

EDITED

BY JUSTIN WINSOR
LIBRARIAN OF HARVARD UNIVERSITY
CORRESPONDING SECRETARY MASSACHUSETTS HISTORICAL SOCIETY

VOL. I

BOSTON AND NEW YORK
HOUGHTON, MIFFLIN AND COMPANY
The Riverside Press, Cambridge
1889

19 In 1884, thirty-five years after he had launched his career as historian during his freshman year at Harvard by publishing his *History of the Town of Duxbury*, Justin Winsor issued the first of the eight volumes of a *Narrative and Critical History of America*. (Under the plan of publication adopted for the set, Volume I, relating to "Aboriginal America," was the last to be issued, in 1889.)

This was not an American history on a larger scale than any other of its time, but it was the first major collaborative undertaking in the subject; there were thirty-nine contributors, though Winsor wrote about half of the work. It was distinguished also by his aim. Its "main purpose," Winsor wrote, "was to set forth a bibliographical and critical record of all the sources of the history of the American continent. . . ."

Clearly he was concerned less with creating a literary monument than with producing a guide, a map that would help other historians to continue exploration on their own. He was highly successful, for his work is still useful after nearly a century. In Channing's judgment, he "made the scientific study of American history possible by making available the rich mines of material."

Perhaps this aim was to be expected of a great historian who was also a great librarian. Winsor's administration as the librarian of Harvard for twenty years (following nine years as head of the Boston Public Library) was noteworthy above all for his efforts to make the collections accessible. President Eliot of Harvard said that he "was the first librarian I ever saw whose fundamental policy, never lost sight of for a moment, was to get books used, even though they should be used up."

Unusual though the policy seemed to Eliot, it is the policy that has prevailed in most American libraries throughout the past century, and Winsor, as first president of the American Library Association, from 1876 to 1885, was among those who did the most to make it prevail.

Cartography, the third field in which Winsor distinguished himself, was closely related to the two others. He built up a great historical map collection at Harvard, and "history and geography commingled" in his writings, Horace Scudder observed, "with geographical evolution the backbone of the structure."

Few men have served scholarship as well as Justin Winsor, and few books have been as useful to historians as his *Narrative and Critical History of America*.

DOUGLAS W. BRYANT
Director, Harvard University Library

HISTORY

OF THE

UNITED STATES

FROM

THE COMPROMISE OF 1850

BY

JAMES FORD RHODES

VOL. I
1850–1854

NEW YORK
HARPER & BROTHERS PUBLISHERS
1893

20

In 1893, James Ford Rhodes emerged suddenly as a major historian and interpreter of the Civil War. His first two volumes, published in that year, were followed by five more at intervals during the next fourteen years, climaxing his lengthy chronicle with the restoration of Southern home rule in 1877. It was a stunning and moving narrative, weaving together the major political and military themes of perhaps the most important era since the founding of the republic.

Rhodes was an unlikely historian. Born and bred to industrial and political Ohio, he grew up in Cleveland and succeeded to his father's iron and coal business, which commanded his attention and energies until he was in his mid-thirties. His university education had been perfunctory, and he gave little evidence of the scholarly capabilities he later developed. In 1885, at the age of thirty-seven, he sold his business to his brother-in-law, Mark Hanna, and embarked on his second, and great, career.

In retrospect Rhodes's reckless self-confidence appears characteristically American. The nation had already grown accustomed to self-made men in business and politics, but the scholarly world was another milieu—the preserve of well-born aristocrats steeped in academic traditions. Armed with considerable wealth, Rhodes scaled the walls of Brahmin Boston, and by his warmth as well as his scholarship won acceptance to the ranks of distinguished authors for whom history was a lifetime profession: Prescott, Parkman, and Bancroft.

Rhodes's *History* was fortunately timed, for it served to evoke nostalgia for a war still fresh in the minds of older men and to soothe the still-unhealed wounds of conflict. However, these qualities alone would not have insured the durability of his work. Moral fervor wedded to intense patriotism gave his history a lofty tone and made the American imperative seem unassailable at the very moment the nation was embarking upon the completion of its "manifest destiny."

Flawed though his narrative is by its failure to embrace the economic elements in the Civil War and by its Northern bias, his perception of the events as a contest between good and evil was in the greatest tradition of historical writing up to that time, and he overcame all criticisms of the experts, including Woodrow Wilson's.

Rhodes, even at this date, has much of importance to say to us of our history, but he also unconsciously illuminates much of the American psyche. He is representative of a significant cultural development in our past.

Ervin J. Gaines
Director, Cleveland Public Library

HISTORY

OF THE

UNITED STATES OF AMERICA

DURING THE FIRST ADMINISTRATION OF

THOMAS JEFFERSON

By HENRY ADAMS

Vol. I.

NEW YORK
CHARLES SCRIBNER'S SONS
1889

21

The great-grandson of John Adams, the grandson of John Quincy Adams, and the son of Charles Francis Adams was born on Beacon Hill in the city of Boston. But it was as a longtime resident in Washington, D.C., later in his career, that Henry Adams devoted much of his time to the writing of history. Following the death of his wife, in 1885, Adams began the task of completing his *History of the United States of America*.

The first two volumes, covering Jefferson's first administration, were published in 1889. The second administration of Jefferson and the first of Madison were covered in the next four volumes, published in 1890. In 1891, the last three volumes, on the second administration of Madison, were published.

In the words of Henry Steele Commager, written forty years after the publication of the first two volumes, the *History*, which placed Henry Adams in the first rank of American historians, is "not only a literary achievement of rare beauty, but an historical achievement of the first order."

Commager speaks of "the limpid clarity and beauty, the classic restraint, the flashing brilliance of the prose; the lofty and tranquil impartiality, rigidly judicious without being abstract or impersonal; the serene philosophic approach which permeates the grave unhurried pages of the volumes; the fine sense of balance and form that distinguishes the work of art from a mere compilation of historical facts; the splendid devotion to, the rigorous regard for, truth as the ultimate end of history."

The first six chapters of the first volume are noteworthy in their description of economic, social, and intellectual conditions in the United States at the turn of the century. Adams had a first-hand acquaintance with the documentary material in foreign archives. This, plus his personal mastery of the diplomatic background of the period, gives his writing an authoritative character.

In essence, Adams' *History* marks one of the highest achievements in American historiography.

JOHN G. LORENZ
Executive Director, Association of Research Libraries

THE

WINNING OF THE WEST

BY

THEODORE ROOSEVELT

AUTHOR OF "NAVAL WAR OF 1812," "LIFE OF THOMAS HART BENTON," "LIFE OF GOUVERNEUR MORRIS," "HUNTING TRIPS OF A RANCHMAN," "RANCH LIFE AND THE HUNTING TRAIL," "ESSAYS ON PRACTICAL POLITICS," ETC.

VOLUME I.

FROM THE ALLEGHANIES TO THE MISSISSIPPI

1769-1776

NEW YORK AND LONDON

G. P. PUTNAM'S SONS

The Knickerbocker Press

1889

22

Although a number of Presidents of the United States have written memoirs and Thomas Jefferson authored a celebrated volume entitled *Notes on the State of Virginia*, only two of our chief executives can truly be classed as having been historians, Theodore Roosevelt and Woodrow Wilson.

Before his entry into public affairs, Theodore Roosevelt wrote *The Winning of the West*, which was published between 1889 and 1896 in four volumes. Roosevelt's West is the land between the Appalachians and the Mississippi, for he did not fulfill his intention to carry the expansion of the United States into Florida, Texas, and Oregon. His prose epic recounts the endless encounters, from 1770 until 1800, between the British and the Indians, on one side, and the American backwoodsmen, on the other.

As a patriotic American who had lived on a later frontier, Roosevelt's sympathies lie always with the "true borderers—brave, self-reliant, loyal to their friends and good hearted."

His prose often is highly colored and, at its best, achieves eloquence: "With moccasined feet they [the Indians] trod among brittle twigs, dried leaves, and dead branches as silently as the cougar, and they equalled the great wood-cat in stealth and far surpassed it in cunning and ferocity." In his thirties, Roosevelt foreshadowed the President who carried a Big Stick and "took" Panama: "Americans need to keep in mind the fact that as a nation they have erred far more often in not being willing to fight than in being too willing."

More than three years after he had left the White House, former-President Roosevelt became president of the American Historical Association, an organization of professional historians whom he once characterized as "day laborers." In his presidential address, "History as Literature," Roosevelt called for more imaginative treatments and strong moral judgments. Facts and the perceptions provided by other disciplines should be employed to portray the lives of plain people, and the true historian "will bring the past before our eyes as if it were the present."

These are qualities to be found in rich abundance in Roosevelt's *The Winning of the West*; at times they elevate and at times they mar his pages.

LESLIE W. DUNLAP
Dean of Library Administration, University of Iowa

GUIDE

TO THE STUDY OF

AMERICAN HISTORY

BY

EDWARD CHANNING, Ph.D.
AND
ALBERT BUSHNELL HART, Ph.D.

ASSISTANT PROFESSORS OF HISTORY IN
HARVARD UNIVERSITY

BOSTON, U.S.A., AND LONDON
GINN & COMPANY, PUBLISHERS
The Athenæum Press
1896

23

At the end of the 19th Century an increasing number of scholars were turning to the careful, scientific study of American history. In the forefront of the professionalization of history teaching and writing were two Harvard professors, Edward Channing and Albert Bushnell Hart, who lectured to large undergraduate classes and for several years jointly taught a graduate seminar. In 1896 they published a small handbook, *Guide to the Study of American History*, incorporating the materials they had developed in the seminar.

This outline and basic bibliography for a course in American history to 1865 had a major influence on the teaching of history in colleges and secondary schools.

Channing and Hart, so effective in stimulating the study of history, were not an entirely compatible pair. Channing, born in 1856, the descendant of eminent New Englanders, was a notable teacher and textbook writer, but soon husbanded his time outside the classroom to write a distinguished multi-volume history of the United States. Hart, born in 1854 and raised in Cleveland, after studying at Harvard took a doctorate in Germany. President Charles Eliot appointed him at Harvard to develop the field of American history, and so he did with his lively, popular lectures, his personal ebullience, and his prolific writing and editing. He was editor of the influential "American Nation" series.

The *Guide* was so successful that in 1912 Channing and Hart brought out an enlarged edition, associating with them Frederick Jackson Turner, the historian of the frontier, who had joined the Harvard faculty.

In the 1920s the next generation of Harvard historians began a thorough revision of the *Guide*, which finally resulted, under the principal editorship of Oscar Handlin, in the basically new and far larger *Harvard Guide to American History* (1953). A score of years later, in 1974, a still further revision, this time in two volumes, reflected the continued growth and vitality of the American historical scholarship that Channing and Hart had nurtured in its beginnings.

FRANK FREIDEL
Charles Warren Professor of American History,
Harvard University;
Editor, "Harvard Guide to American History" (1974)

The Literary History

OF THE

American Revolution

1763–1783

BY

MOSES COIT TYLER

Professor of American History in Cornell University

VOLUME I.
1763–1776

G. P. PUTNAM'S SONS

NEW YORK   LONDON
27 WEST TWENTY-THIRD STREET   24 BEDFORD STREET, STRAND

The Knickerbocker Press

1897

24

The social purpose which stirred Moses Coit Tyler to write, first, his *A History of American Literature, 1607–1765* (published in 1878) and, then, *The Literary History of the American Revolution* (1897) has sustained their influence through several generations of scholars. His intent in the latter, as he says in his preface, to examine not the "principal movers and doers," but the "persons who . . . nourished the springs of great historic events by creating and shaping and directing public opinion during all that robust time . . . who still illustrate for us and for all who choose to see, the majestic operation of ideas, the creative and decisive play of spiritual forces, in the development of history, in the rise and fall of nations, in the aggregation and the division of races," anticipated the social and intellectual historians who shortly followed him.

Interpreting literature in terms of social and political influence and of its usefulness to society was a contribution to American literary criticism that Tyler as an historian was uniquely equipped to make. He went to Cornell University in 1881 and there occupied the first professorship in American history in the United States. And it was at Cornell that he wrote his *Literary History of the American Revolution*.

Although the *Literary History* is a landmark of scholarship and stands—through its originality of purpose, as well as its analysis and expression—as a major piece of American literature and American historical writing, it was also a work for consultation and reference. It so served generations of students and teachers and it continues to serve them.

The comprehensive *Cambridge History of American Literature* is larger in scope and extent and is certainly the authoritative reference text for the whole subject, yet it by no means supersedes Tyler's work. The perceptions of how letters, pamphlets, books, and essays expressed the strength and passions of the Americans of both sides during the Revolution, and stirred and influenced the events that took place, still provide the strong yet balanced background that students and teachers can turn to for fact, stimulation, and insight.

J. GORMLY MILLER
Director of Libraries, Cornell University

THE THEORY OF
THE LEISURE CLASS

*AN ECONOMIC STUDY IN THE EVOLUTION
OF INSTITUTIONS*

BY

THORSTEIN VEBLEN

New York
THE MACMILLAN COMPANY
LONDON: MACMILLAN & CO., Ltd.
1899

All rights reserved

25

Until the middle of this century the reputable American economics and much of our sociology were imported, primarily from Britain. Smith, Ricardo, the Mills, Alfred Marshall were the economic names of distinction. All the best-regarded American work was derived from them. No sociologist in the last century had such influence in the United States as Herbert Spencer.

Standing as exceptions were two uniquely American writers, both men of the frontier—Henry George and Thorstein Veblen. Both are still read, George by a cult, Veblen for the most amusing and uncompromising studies ever made of the economics and sociology of wealth.

Veblen was born of Norwegian immigrant parents in 1857, raised on a Minnesota farm, had his first education at local schools and a small nearby seminary, now Carleton College, went on to Johns Hopkins and Yale. (He taught variously and briefly at several universities, died in 1929.) It's a mark of the American inferiority complex that many thought it remarkable that so great a figure could have had such commonplace, even bucolic origins. His background, peculiarly American with its democratic and egalitarian ethos, goes far, in fact, to explain both the Veblen motivation and the Veblen achievement.

The Theory of the Leisure Class, Veblen's first and greatest book, was published in the closing months of the last century. From it come terms—Conspicuous Consumption, Conspicuous Leisure, the Predatory Culture—that recur to this day. It helped change the manners of a whole society. Ostentatious display of wealth ceased to be an unqualified mark of distinction; it became instead a subject of slighting comment, even ridicule. And enough doubt was cast on the means by which wealth was accumulated to pave the way for the income and inheritance taxes that at least moderated the accumulation.

JOHN KENNETH GALBRAITH
Paul M. Warburg Professor of Economics Emeritus,
Harvard University;
Author, "The Affluent Society"

Two Centuries of Costume in America

MDCXX — MDCCCXX

BY

ALICE MORSE EARLE

AUTHOR OF "SUN-DIALS AND ROSES OF YESTERDAY"
"OLD TIME GARDENS," ETC.

VOLUME I

New York
The Macmillan Company
London: Macmillan & Co., Ltd.
Nineteen Hundred and Three.   *All rights reserved*

26

Alice Morse Earle's *Two Centuries of Costume in America* is more than a history of American costume between 1620 and 1820, for its pages are full of manners, morals, scandals, gossip, and domestic history relating to both American and English life. The pleasant garrulity may detract from its value as a treatise, but it has the advantage of pleasing the reader with an eye for entertainment.

Historically the book is of value for recounting some of the interesting facts that obtained, such as: during this period Americans, as a class, dressed more expensively and fashionably than Englishmen; men were as fashion conscious as women; Puritans thought much of style, and their dress was not of "sad color" but included browns, russet, purple, orange, and green.

We find that although the dress of the Puritans and Cavaliers differed little in quality, quantity, cost, or form, the rich and poor of each dressed very differently. The vanity of our respected first settlers is quite surprising; many borrowed clothes to sit for portraits, and even cajoled the artist into plastering them with jewels and gold. (It would seem that immediately on landing, they plumped right down on Plymouth Rock and began making lists of fashionable garments they would need for the life in the wilderness, and both male and female kept on sending back, to the England they had spurned, for fashionable attire.)

The mass of material taken from household accounts, tailors' bills, estate inventories, letters, diaries, photographs, and portraits is astonishing. Nothing has been left out that has clothed the human frame since the 17th Century, for every kind of costume and its various parts—even the dressing of hair, wigs, beards, jewelry, and christening garments—is well described, and illustrated with more than three hundred and fifty examples.

One can revel in all the gorgeousness of historic American finery, from the beautiful Van Dyck costumes and the plainer dress of the Quakers and Puritans, through the ornateness of Restoration times, to the scantiness of Empire fashions.

Mrs. Earle's books (about fifteen) fostered the renewed interest in our Colonial past which developed near the close of the 19th Century, and because she wrote in an entertaining fashion her books had a considerable sale. This two-volume work, published in 1903, with a new edition in 1910, can be considered the author's most significant production.

GLENORA EDWARDS ROSSELL
Director, University of Pittsburgh Libraries

AMERICAN BIBLIOGRAPHY

BY

CHARLES EVANS

A CHRONOLOGICAL DICTIONARY

OF ALL

BOOKS, PAMPHLETS AND PERIODICAL PUBLICATIONS

PRINTED IN THE

UNITED STATES OF AMERICA

FROM THE GENESIS OF PRINTING IN 1639
DOWN TO AND INCLUDING THE YEAR 1820

WITH BIBLIOGRAPHICAL AND BIOGRAPHICAL NOTES

VOLUME I
1639-1729

Da mihi, Domine, scire quod sciendum est!—Thomas à Kempis
Look, Lucius, here's the book I sought for so.—Shakespeare

PRIVATELY PRINTED FOR THE AUTHOR
BY THE BLAKELY PRESS, CHICAGO
ANNO DOMINI MDCCCCIII

27

This pioneer work of Charles Evans could well be designated the Plymouth Rock of American bibliography, except this fails to give a fair impression of its author's vision, ruthless and ironlike determination, seemingly endless energy, and attention to every detail of his undertaking—which by the time of his death in 1935 was the Gibraltar of bibliography in this country.

In 1866 Evans joined the staff at the Boston Athenæum, aged sixteen. (Orphaned at nine, he had been placed in the Boston Farm and Trade School, where he was befriended by Dr. Samuel Eliot, Boston educator, philanthropist, and trustee of the Athenæum.) At the time of Evans' appointment, the librarian was one of the major figures of early American library history, William F. Poole, and Poole took particular interest in developing young assistants along professional lines.

Unable to obtain the college education he so desired, Evans through contact with the Athenæum's collections, staff, and readers secured a more truly liberal education than he might have obtained at a college in his time. In turn, he gratefully dedicated the second volume of his work to the "president, trustees, proprietors, and library officials of the Boston Athenæum of thirty-five years ago, the alma mater of my bibliographical life, and to their successors of to-day. . . ."

Having early conceived the idea of his American bibliography, recording the titles of all examples of printing in this country from 1639 through 1820, Evans (after a turbulent subsequent career) in 1901 began serious work on the undertaking. In 1903 the first volume appeared.

Though he had the assistance of friends and patrons from time to time, it was Evans' complete absorption and his patient self-sacrificing labors, over many years, which enabled him to put at the disposal of scholars and librarians "one of the most valuable works of reference ever produced." All the manuscript of his bibliography was prepared in his own handwriting, and each and every detail of the printing was personally considered and overseen by him. Even the indexes were entirely his own work.

Evans did not reach his goal, for he was working on the thirteenth volume, which would have taken the record to 1800, at his death—though his task has since been taken up by others.

RODNEY ARMSTRONG
Director and Librarian, Boston Athenæum

LIBRARY OF CONGRESS

JOURNALS OF THE CONTINENTAL CONGRESS

1774-1789

EDITED FROM THE ORIGINAL RECORDS
IN THE LIBRARY OF CONGRESS BY
WORTHINGTON CHAUNCEY FORD
CHIEF, DIVISION OF MANUSCRIPTS

Volume I. 1774

WASHINGTON
GOVERNMENT PRINTING OFFICE
1904

28

In the summer of 1902, Worthington Chauncey Ford became the second chief of the Division of Manuscripts of the Library of Congress. The following year, in March 1903, President Theodore Roosevelt's executive order transferred to the library—and thereby to Ford's official custody—important historical papers then housed in the Department of State, including the records of the Continental Congress. It was to be a classic meeting of the man and the muniment.

Ford was familiar with the historical archive from his service in the State Department as chief of its Bureau of Statistics, 1885–89. His proposal at that time to edit the papers of the founding fathers was transmitted to Congress by President Cleveland in 1888. Failing to win Congressional support, Ford undertook his own edition of Washington's *Writings*, published in fourteen volumes, 1889–93.

The first volume of W. C. Ford's edition of *Journals of the Continental Congress* was published by the Library of Congress in 1904. The edition eventually required thirty-four volumes, the last published in 1937. The extraordinary Ford edited the first fifteen volumes at the rate of three per year. His successor in the Manuscript Division, Gaillard Hunt, edited volumes sixteen through twenty-seven (1910–28), and the project was brought to completion (1933–37) under the direction of J. Franklin Jameson, who followed Hunt.

Other significant historical and documentary publications were prepared in the library's Manuscript Division before World War II. The *Journals*, however, was, in Edmund C. Burnett's phrase, the "noble enterprise" in the group.

The importance of the journals is inestimable. The principles of national existence were formulated in the proceedings which they record. Until the Library of Congress publication, however, the journals had not been published in full, supplemented by relevant original sources of the period.

In 1908 Ford moved to the Massachusetts Historical Society, where for twenty years he was responsible for a series of distinguished historical volumes. He then re-associated himself with the Library of Congress and moved to Europe, to further the Manuscript Division's program to photocopy historical sources in European archives. In 1940, following the German occupation, the octogenarian Ford made his escape from France but died at sea, early in 1941, en route to the United States.

The manuscript records of the Continental Congress subsequently were transferred to the National Archives, where they now repose.

JOHN C. BRODERICK
Chief, Manuscript Division, Library of Congress

THE HISTORY OF
THE STANDARD OIL COMPANY

BY

IDA M. TARBELL

AUTHOR OF
THE LIFE OF ABRAHAM LINCOLN, THE LIFE OF NAPOLEON BONAPARTE,
AND MADAME ROLAND: A BIOGRAPHICAL STUDY

ILLUSTRATED WITH PORTRAITS
PICTURES AND DIAGRAMS

VOLUME ONE

NEW YORK
McCLURE, PHILLIPS & CO.
MCMIV

29

Broad vision, financial acumen, and cut-throat competition characterized the spectacular growth of post–Civil War big business in the United States. Between 1902 and 1912 a group of writers, including Lincoln Steffens, Ray Stannard Baker, Ida Tarbell, and Mark Sullivan, began to expose the whited sepulchres among the country's revered models of business and political success, in new popular-priced magazines like *McClure's* and *Cosmopolitan*. They wrote with varying degrees of thoroughness and objectivity, for a rapidly growing group of readers. Angry at their excesses, Theodore Roosevelt called them "muckrakers," after the muckraker in *Pilgrim's Progress*; nevertheless, they helped to create widespread support for the trust-busting reforms of his Progressive Movement.

The editor of *McClure's* magazine asked Ida M. Tarbell, already famous for biographies of Napoleon and Lincoln, to write the story of that emerging colossus, the Standard Oil Company, and her *History of the Standard Oil Company* first appeared as a series of articles (1902–04). Its obvious thoroughness and meticulous documentation commanded general respect. Moreover, it had immense and immediate moral impact, because it was plainly and fervently written by an avowed daughter of the Pennsylvania oil fields, deeply troubled by the plight of small oil producers.

Miss Tarbell praised the Standard as a model of efficiency and organization, but condemned it for systematically and unlawfully stifling competition and controlling prices in the oil business in order to realize excessive profits. Further, she maintained that if these illegal and unethical practices were perceived as essential to business success, there would be no such thing as "fair play" in the business community. This she regarded as a threat to the general welfare.

By profession a journalist, Miss Tarbell has been described as a "scholar by inclination and a research historian by training." She was also a humanist whose early scientific bent gave her a solid respect for facts. This unique combination of temperament, training, and experience produced in *The History of the Standard Oil Company* what Allan Nevins has called "the most spectacular success of the muckraking school, and its most enduring achievement."

PAGE ACKERMAN
University Librarian, University of California, Los Angeles

Early Western Travels
1748-1846

A Series of Annotated Reprints of some of the best and rarest contemporary volumes of travel, descriptive of the Aborigines and Social and Economic Conditions in the Middle and Far West, during the Period of Early American Settlement

Edited with Notes, Introductions, Index, etc., by

Reuben Gold Thwaites

Editor of "The Jesuit Relations and Allied Documents," "Wisconsin Historical Collections," "Chronicles of Border Warfare," "Hennepin's New Discovery," etc.

Volume I
Journals of
Conrad Weiser (1748), George Croghan (1750-1765)
Christian Frederick Post (1758), and
Thomas Morris (1764)

Cleveland, Ohio
The Arthur H. Clark Company
1904

30

The major interest of Reuben Gold Thwaites, historian and editor, was the story of human achievement. His *Early Western Travels*, published 1904–07, brings together in thirty-two volumes one saga of man's progress, the early settlement of Western America. Opening with an account of the journey in 1748 of the first official Colonial envoy to the Indian tribes west of the Alleghenies, and closing with the journal of Joel Palmer, a pioneer who joined the 1845 settlement of Oregon, Thwaites' narrative, as one reviewer wrote, "is not merely useful to the historian, but filled with tales of such strange and thrilling adventure as to hold the attention of the veriest schoolboy."

The *Travels* was but one of the works Thwaites edited to preserve and make accessible documents from America's early history. Thwaites' edition of *Jesuit Relations* in seventy-three volumes (1896–1901) has come to be considered the definitive edition of these chronicles of American exploration of New France. In the eight-volume first edition of the *Original Journals of Lewis & Clark*, Thwaites completed the journals of this monumental Western expedition and published them in their original format.

More than a man of letters, Thwaites was a librarian, scholar, and administrator of great talent. Born in Massachusetts in 1853, as a young man he moved to Wisconsin. For twenty-five years as secretary of the State Historical Society of Wisconsin, Thwaites guided the growth of the society's collections; his scientific spirit and progressive attitude combined to make a library of outstanding reputation.

In 1900 as president of the American Library Association he shared with his colleagues his vision of the library as a democratic institution and a "common heritage of all our people."

On Thwaites' death in 1913, Frederick Jackson Turner remembered him as "a great organizer of historical industry," a man who "left an indelible impress . . . upon the historical activities of the nation," and whose "life tells a story so rich in achievement, usefulness, and service that it is an inspiration."

CLARA S. JONES
President, American Library Association

DEPARTMENT OF COMMERCE AND LABOR
BUREAU OF THE CENSUS
S. N. D. NORTH, DIRECTOR

A CENTURY OF POPULATION GROWTH

FROM THE FIRST CENSUS OF THE UNITED STATES TO THE TWELFTH
1790–1900

WASHINGTON
GOVERNMENT PRINTING OFFICE
1909

31

Between 1907 and 1908 the Bureau of the Census published in twelve volumes the extant records of the names of heads of families as determined in the first federal census, 1790, "in order permanently to preserve the valuable but vanishing census records which still remain."

This 1909 volume, *A Century of Population Growth*, was seen as a special and final one, designed to discuss the historical aspects of the first census and to present the statistics that could be compiled from existing records. The book, which was prepared by William Sidney Rossiter when he was chief clerk of the bureau, gained added importance in that it provided statistical material for the first time on the condition of the country in 1790, and in that the returns of the first census were compared with corresponding figures from the later censuses, and even with figures from the Colonial period. The result is a fairly complete survey of the population of the United States from the early Colonial times to the time of the nation's twelfth census in 1900.

In his treatment of the population of the Colonial and Continental periods, Rossiter provided valuable tables on such subjects as the estimated population from 1610 to 1790 and the population of the cities from 1656 to 1790. Chapter II ("The United States in 1790") provided especially interesting material, as of 1790, on boundaries, area, currency, transportation, postal service, industries, education, newspapers and periodicals, and the Indians. A valuable and attractive feature of the volume as a whole was the inclusion of reproduction of maps that were already rare in 1900.

Among the chapters containing analyses of the population from 1790 to 1900, there are two of particular interest: Chapter X ("Surnames in the White Population in 1790") and Chapter XI ("Nationality as Indicated by Means of Heads of Families Reported at the First Census"). Some difficulties arose from the way Rossiter derived statistics of national origin from family surnames as returned in 1790, especially as applied to later laws restricting European immigration. His estimates were corrected and improved in the early 1930s.

For the student of American population in particular, this volume stands as a major and pioneer effort to provide an overview, with statistics, of the first census and subsequent censuses through the twelfth. There is a special place for this work among Census Bureau publications and among specialized histories of the United States.

RICHARD L. O'KEEFFE
University Librarian, Rice University

THE CONSERVATION
OF NATURAL RESOURCES

IN THE UNITED STATES

BY

CHARLES RICHARD VAN HISE

MADISON, WISCONSIN

ILLUSTRATED

New York
THE MACMILLAN COMPANY
1910

All rights reserved

32

Student, professor of metallurgy and geology, and finally president of the University of Wisconsin and proponent of "the Wisconsin Idea" (service of the university to the people of the state), Charles R. Van Hise was one in the great continuum of conservationists stretching from John Quincy Adams, through Theodore Roosevelt and Gifford Pinchot, to Aldo Leopold and beyond. His boyhood in rural Wisconsin had convinced him of the need to husband natural resources, and he carried this attitude into manhood, associating himself with state and national conservation groups.

Before the movement had gained popular support, Van Hise became acquainted with the men who brought it forward, and he became himself one of its most energetic leaders. He was a member of the National Conservation Commission and of Theodore Roosevelt's famous White House Conservation Conference of 1908 (termed the most distinguished assemblage in American history since the Constitutional Convention), emphasizing in all his contacts the efficient use of natural resources and the importance of the principle of public control.

Based on a series of lectures at the University of Wisconsin, his book *The Conservation of Natural Resources in the United States* (1910) was the first popular presentation of the value of and the need for conservation of our natural resources. It assumed almost immediately a unique status as the Bible of the conservationists, and it sustained the movement for generations.

In his preface Van Hise wrote, "It is my hope that this book may serve a useful purpose in forwarding the great movement for conservation which, as it seems to me from the point of view of the not distant future of the human race, is more important than all other movements before the people."

The book dealt with conservation of minerals, water, forests, the land—their relationship one with another, to political economy, to legislation, and to mankind itself. It fostered Van Hise's belief that the state should assure development of natural resources without waste: that it should encourage capital in utilizing these resources and, at the same time, protect the people's heritage from exploitation and unfair monopoly.

A seminal work, *The Conservation of Natural Resources in the United States* became the indispensable tool of the student of conservation and the concern of thinking Americans who came to agree with Van Hise that conservation of resources "is by far the most fundamental question before the nation . . . [to which] all political and social questions are subordinate."

JOSEPH H. TREYZ
Director of Libraries, University of Wisconsin, Madison

AN ECONOMIC INTERPRETATION OF THE CONSTITUTION OF THE UNITED STATES

BY

CHARLES A. BEARD
ASSOCIATE PROFESSOR OF POLITICS IN
COLUMBIA UNIVERSITY

New York
THE MACMILLAN COMPANY
1913

All rights reserved

33

Charles Beard's *An Economic Interpretation of the Constitution of the United States* is one of the most provocative, controversial, and influential books ever published in American history. It tarnished a sacred symbol, for it argued that the American Constitution was not so much a product of patriotic idealism as an instrument of special interests—the work of rich men, as against "the propertyless masses" who were "excluded at the outset from participation."

Beard's work was greeted with vehement denunciation when it first appeared (1913), but with the passage of time his thesis found wide scholarly acceptance. The storm of outrage died, and the nation proved to be more than capable of surviving the desacralization of one of its great symbols; the Constitution continued to prove its effectiveness as an instrument of change in stability.

An Economic Interpretation was only the first of several iconoclastic works by Charles Beard. He came by his skepticism and independence honestly. His Quaker grandfather had hidden fugitive slaves in North Carolina, and his father had had to flee to Indiana because of his Unionist sentiments during the Civil War.

Charles Beard himself went to a Quaker school and was exposed in college, both in the United States and in England, to the full range of social criticism and political idealism. His intellectual and political life was, in effect, a working out of these earlier speculations and dreams; it also was an expression of an irrepressible tendency to swim against the stream.

It is no accident that he resigned his post as professor at Columbia in protest against refusal of promotion to anti-war members of the faculty in 1917 or that he found himself drawn into politics in the 1930s on the side of isolationism, in spite of his deep democratic convictions. It is one of the ironies of his career that this liberal, idealistic man should have done his best to prevent America's contribution to the war against the very fascism that he himself hated so much.

He died in 1948, still a major intellectual figure. It was not until about 1950 that his *Economic Interpretation* was subjected to systematic investigation and analysis. These have not been kind to it: little of the thesis remains intact, as a result. But the importance of the book remains undiminished. It is the sort of classic that good teachers assign to their students not to tell them history "as it really was," but to get them to think about it and try to understand it.

DAVID S. LANDES
President, Economic History Association

HISTORY OF LABOUR IN THE UNITED STATES

BY

JOHN R. COMMONS
DAVID J. SAPOSS   HELEN L. SUMNER
E. B. MITTELMAN   H. E. HOAGLAND
JOHN B. ANDREWS   SELIG PERLMAN

WITH AN INTRODUCTORY NOTE
BY
HENRY W. FARNAM

VOLUME I

New York
THE MACMILLAN COMPANY
1918
All rights reserved

34

John R. Commons was interested in social reforms for American society, especially in the labor field. After twelve years of intensive research he, his colleagues, and his students at the University of Wisconsin finished the first complete work on American labor history. The *History of Labour in the United States* consists of four volumes. The first two volumes (1918) cover the Colonial period to the 1890s; the two volumes published in 1935 conclude the history with the New Deal period.

The significance of this classic work has no bounds. It is particularly rich as a source of information for the early years of labor history, when workers were striving to be heard. This history has influenced the thinking of students of labor history and continues to be a source for contemporary writing. Professor Commons' ideas regarding the nature of the labor movement are relevant today. The *History of Labour in the United States* is the greatest contribution made so far in American labor history.

John R. Commons sponsored numerous far-reaching proposals for social legislation. He promoted reforms that benefited both workers and employers. Starting in Wisconsin, he advanced laws relating to industrial relations, such as unemployment compensation, minimum-wage law for women, improved child-labor law. He created Wisconsin's Industrial Commission and generated other reforms that spread to other states and the national government. He contributed greatly to the betterment of our economic life.

The *History of Labour in the United States* was one of a number of special studies sponsored by the Carnegie Institution, studies that included Emory R. Johnson's *History of Domestic and Foreign Commerce of the United States* (1915), Victor S. Clark's *History of Manufactures in the United States* (1916–28), and Balthasar Meyer's *History of Transportation in the United States* (1917).

JEAN Y. WEBBER
Librarian, American Federation of Labor and Congress of Industrial Organizations

AMERICAN NEGRO SLAVERY

A SURVEY OF THE SUPPLY, EMPLOYMENT AND CONTROL OF NEGRO LABOR AS DETERMINED BY THE PLANTATION RÉGIME

BY
ULRICH BONNELL PHILLIPS, Ph.D.
PROFESSOR OF AMERICAN HISTORY IN THE UNIVERSITY OF MICHIGAN

D. APPLETON AND COMPANY
NEW YORK   LONDON
1918

35

This landmark study, still important today, went to the actual records of the Southern plantations and concluded that slavery in America was not the cruel system portrayed in anti-slavery literature. Phillips believed that the plantation was more a way of life than an economic condition, a community in which the influence of the slaves on the masters was very great, resulting most often in a paternalistic feeling on the part of the master, not one of hard or cruel exploitation.

Phillips contributed more to our understanding of plantation life than anyone else and related his discussion to the economic, social, and political conditions of the ante-bellum South. This thorough study by an outstanding historian "made it possible," in the words of Prof. Stanley Elkins, "for the subject to be debated on scholarly grounds."

The debate has extended our understanding of the black American's heritage, his life in slavery, and his present condition in American society as a result of these forces. Kenneth M. Stampp's *The Peculiar Institution* (1956) showed what it was like to be a slave, and took issue with Phillips' assumption of Negro inferiority, as well as his conclusion that the plantation system, on the whole, treated the slave well and culturally benefited him. Edward F. Frazier's *The Negro in the United States* (1949) traced the slow integration of the Negro into American society to the present time. Margaret Butcher's *The Negro in American Culture* (1956) examined the Negro's contribution to American literature, drama, music, dance, and the visual arts.

Though some of Phillips' opinions have been revised, his work has been the point of departure and the challenge to excellence for these and subsequent studies so important to an understanding of the difficult transition of the black man into American life.

Ulrich B. Phillips was born in La Grange, Georgia, in 1877 and died suddenly, at the height of his powers, in 1934 while working on a three-volume history of the South. He held professorships at the University of Wisconsin, Tulane, the University of Michigan, and Yale.

He was acknowledged by his colleagues to be the greatest authority of his time on the life of the Cotton Belt prior to the Civil War. His writing style, lucid and straightforward, carried the drama of his sources with telling force. His personal library of source materials was remarkable, and at his death he left one of the finest collections of Southern history in existence.

RAY W. FRANTZ JR.
University Librarian, University of Virginia

THE
AMERICAN LANGUAGE

A Preliminary Inquiry into the Development of English in the United States

BY

H. L. MENCKEN

NEW YORK
ALFRED · A · KNOPF
MCMXIX

36

We owe many debts to H. L. Mencken, but I think the one that will remain with us the longest is a discovery he published first in 1919, that Americans do not speak English—they have a language of their own which, for the want of a better name, he called "American." Mr. Mencken was very intrigued with the language, possibly because he lived in Baltimore where Southern and Northern dialects seemed to crash against each other with such force that a newspaperman had to ask everyone he spoke with to repeat everything he said twice, to make sure he got it right.

We can only speculate as to why Mr. Mencken would devote a lifetime to pointing out the differences between "English" and "American." Anyone who has ever visited England (let's forget about Scotland, Wales, and Ireland) knows the English have a crude, unsophisticated gibberish which they have been speaking for thousands of years. It took the Americans less than two hundred years to refine this language and make it understandable as a means of communicating with one another.

Mr. Mencken predicted that in time "English" and "American" would go their own separate ways and become two foreign languages, with very little in common. He was a visionary, because any of us who have heard our teenagers speak their version of "American" know it bears no resemblance to the subject which we called "English" when we went to school. Today's student begins every sentence with "like," as in "Like, I'd like to borrow the car tonight," and finishes every sentence with "y'know," as in "I have to buy another pair of jeans, y'know."

My only regret is that Mr. Mencken isn't around to do another revised edition of *The American Language*. It would have very little resemblance to his previous revised edition. He would not only have to explain the differences between the English and American languages, but the major linguistic changes that have taken place in this country by a generation of children who never learned "English" or "American."

Like, I think it's a task he might have warmed to, though God knows he's the only one, to my knowledge, who would have dared tackle it, y'know.

ART BUCHWALD
Syndicated Newspaper Columnist

THE FRONTIER
IN AMERICAN HISTORY

BY
FREDERICK JACKSON TURNER

NEW YORK
HENRY HOLT AND COMPANY

37

Neither prolific in writing nor dogmatic in presentation, Frederick Jackson Turner became an instant authority, and later a controversial figure, in United States historiography. In 1893, as a young professor, the Wisconsin-born scholar presented his seminal paper, "The Significance of the Frontier in American History," at a special meeting of the American Historical Association held at Chicago's World's Fair. Later this became the lead section of his expanded essays in a volume entitled *The Frontier in American History* (1920).

In considerable measure Turner was responsible for breaking United States history away from its earlier political and military orientation, toward a larger goal of "all the spheres of man's activity." In doing so he became a pioneer of interpretive exposition, rather than writing strictly narrative history of events arranged chronologically.

Departing from standard emphasis, Turner declared that the true point of view in United States history was not the Atlantic Coast, it was the Great West. Certainly, his writings had the effect of broadening history to embrace the West as a genuine part of the national experience, as he clearly delineated the role of the frontier.

Turner never claimed to be a Western historian. He was, as might be expected of his period, a nationalistic, ethnocentric interpreter who sought in the Western experience, which he knew personally and studied avidly, those things which characterized United States civilization, as opposed to its European counterpart.

After his death in 1924, Turner's critics multiplied, chipping away at the basic concept that "The existence of an area of free land, its continuous recession, and the advance of American settlement westward, explain American development"—as well as attacking other sub-theses. Some critics were right, others wrong, but Turner's place as a creative force in national historical writing remains. His ideas, fruit of mature consideration, became the foci of research of others, ranging from bitter critics to staunch disciples.

As to the vitality of Turner's "frontier thesis," one needs only to consult the descriptions of hundreds of course offerings in United States universities and colleges.

DONALD C. CUTTER
President, Western History Association

THE AMERICAN SPIRIT
IN EDUCATION
A CHRONICLE OF
GREAT TEACHERS
BY EDWIN E. SLOSSON

NEW HAVEN: YALE UNIVERSITY PRESS
TORONTO: GLASGOW, BROOK & CO.
LONDON: HUMPHREY MILFORD
OXFORD UNIVERSITY PRESS
1921

38

The American spirit in education is manifest in the development of a system of free public education which provides to any "youth of sufficient ability to profit by opportunity . . . any education he needs, up to the highest professional training without spending any money other than what he can make by his own exertions during his course."

Edwin E. Slosson traces the history of this American spirit in *The American Spirit in Education*. The book is a short, traditional history of education in this country, from its early beginnings in New England through World War I. The story is told around the efforts of a number of great teachers and prophets in American education.

The emphasis is on the development of higher education, with separate chapters on such topics as the Morrill Act, Catholic education in America, the entrance of women into college, and the rise of technical education.

The American Spirit in Education is the thirty-third volume of the series "Chronicles of America," edited by Allen Johnson. The series consists of fifty small volumes, published between 1918 and 1921, whose purpose was "to provide the intelligent general reader with a history of the United States composed of volumes each having a certain unity, readable, yet conforming to high standards of scholarship." Johnson maintained the series at the level he had set for them. All fifty volumes are in print today.

Edwin E. Slosson was well qualified to write a book in this series. He received a Ph.D. degree in chemistry from the University of Chicago in 1902. While still an associate professor at the University of Wyoming, he began to combine journalism with the natural sciences. He later became director of Science Service.

His interests were not limited to the natural sciences; he wrote widely on various cultural topics. Indeed, Rollins College offered him a position with the title of "Professor of Things in General." Unfortunately, he died before he could accept this formidable challenge.

ROGER W. HEYNS
President, American Council on Education

THE SUPREME COURT
IN
UNITED STATES HISTORY

BY

CHARLES WARREN

FORMERLY ASSISTANT ATTORNEY-GENERAL OF THE UNITED STATES
AUTHOR OF "A HISTORY OF THE AMERICAN BAR"

IN THREE VOLUMES
VOLUME ONE
1789–1821

BOSTON
LITTLE, BROWN, AND COMPANY
1922

39

Charles Warren's *The Supreme Court in United States History* is a landmark work in the treatment of the history of the Supreme Court. Published in 1922, the book immediately received critical acclaim, including the Pulitzer Prize for history. No other work of that era rivaled Warren's in its distinction and sophistication—with the exception of a biography: Albert Beveridge's *The Life of John Marshall*, published six years earlier. Over half a century later, Warren's text remains the standard by which to judge histories of the Supreme Court.

Charles Warren (1868-1954) was a distinguished member of the Massachusetts bar and a government official, as well as a scholar and professor of law. In *The Supreme Court in United States History* he avoided the prevalent temptation to write a treatise on constitutional law and produced, instead, an analysis of the Supreme Court as an active, vital element in the American polity, of interest to lawyer and laymen alike.

Warren chose to follow the court year by year, considering each of its important cases in its historical and political context. He was interested, as well, in the justices of the Supreme Court and the controversies over their appointments.

Perhaps the most impressive contribution, however, is the new dimension which Warren added to the written history of the court. Through indefatigable research into newspapers, periodical stories, editorials, political oratory, legislative debate, pamphlets, diaries, and correspondence Warren was able to write authoritatively about the reactions of politicians, the press, and the public to the work of the Supreme Court.

Because Warren did not consider in depth decisions after 1874, we can look forward to the multi-volume Oliver Wendell Holmes Devise *History of the Supreme Court of the United States*, edited by Prof. Paul A. Freund, of which three volumes have thus far been published. The Holmes Devise series will reassess in greater detail the entire period Professor Warren handled so well, plus chronicling the last one hundred years of the Supreme Court.

WARREN E. BURGER
Chief Justice of the United States

STICKS AND STONES

A STUDY OF AMERICAN ARCHITECTURE
AND CIVILIZATION

LEWIS MUMFORD

BONI and LIVERIGHT
PUBLISHERS :: :: NEW YORK

When a book published by an author "under thirty" had already reached its seventh printing in four years, one might well wonder whether such youthful vigor and popularity could endure. Since its appearance in 1924, however, Lewis Mumford's *Sticks and Stones* has remained an eminently readable, informative, and prophetic account of American building up to that time.

Beginning with the Medieval traditions of Colonial days, proceeding through the Renaissance and Classical eras, to the age of eclecticism and the subsequent search for a new architectural identity, the author traced the visual forms as he saw them emerging from social structures changing over the years.

The main impact of his concern was the effect of industrialization, which he recorded as having created inhuman conditions in the cities and having threatened the resources of the countryside. He deplored not so much the machine, in itself, as its misuse in shaping the environment, and he wished for a renewal of the individual values of handicraft.

While in the last chapter he dealt largely with social philosophy, the force of his arguments was carried in the concluding statement that "architecture sums up the civilization it enshrines."

Now, more than half a century later, Professor Mumford's career has borne out its early promise, in a distinguished record of teaching and publication, accompanied by many honors.

What he in 1924 hoped for in betterment of human dwelling conditions has been to only a small degree achieved. His strict, but sensitive and compassionate, sometimes even mischievous, plea for a society that can build for human dignity may still be heard.

MARIAN C. DONNELLY
President, Society of Architectural Historians

THE CLIMATES
OF THE UNITED STATES

BY

ROBERT DeCOURCY WARD

PROFESSOR OF CLIMATOLOGY IN HARVARD UNIVERSITY

GINN AND COMPANY
BOSTON · NEW YORK · CHICAGO · LONDON
ATLANTA · DALLAS · COLUMBUS · SAN FRANCISCO

41 While little, in truth, can presently be done about the weather, it has not only been talked about, but written about at length—from almanacs to erudition—some writings being landmark works in the America of their time. Hugh Williamson's *Observations on the Climate in Different Parts of America* (1811) brought fame and professional plaudits to this statesman and physician. In the mid-19th Century *Climatology of the United States* (1857) was deemed an important compilation, gaining (despite its faults) lasting recognition for statistician Lorin Blodget, a sometime Smithsonian meteorological observer.

Robert DeCourcy Ward, however, is considered to be the first American to make professional climatology his life's work; his Harvard professorship was the first such chair in the United States and one of very few in the world at that time.

In founding and developing his department, Ward was acutely aware of the lack of truly satisfactory educational materials. His career was marked by prodigious efforts to bring together in organized fashion all he could find of the climatological works of others, simplifying and presenting descriptions, arguments, and conclusions in concise, precise terms. Where gaps in the knowledge corpus were apparent, Ward undertook to fill them, through extensive research of his own and the guided research of his students.

His work exhibited here, *The Climates of the United States* (1925), reflected over twenty-five years of this research and teaching. In it are enumerated the seven major climatic controls, a working scheme of eight climatic provinces for the United States, and extensive analyses of such phenomena as frost, temperature, prevailing winds, rainfall, snowfall, and so forth. As in his other writings, Ward professed particular concern with the practical application of climatology to human affairs, and his text is enlivened with allusions to the personal meanings of climatic effects.

The volume retained its authority for over three decades and helped to establish and strengthen professional education in climatology. It was also, as its author intended, of major value "to medical men, to foresters, to agriculturists, as well as to the general public."

First president of the American Meteorological Society, Ward pioneered in seeking the development of climatology as a science in this country. His straightforward, understandable, precise expositions served not only to educate soundly, but contributed much to popularization of the topic in America.

WILLIAM S. BUDINGTON
Executive Director and Librarian, John Crerar Library

THE AMERICAN REVOLUTION CONSIDERED AS A SOCIAL MOVEMENT

BY
J. FRANKLIN JAMESON
DIRECTOR OF THE DEPARTMENT OF HISTORICAL RESEARCH
IN THE CARNEGIE INSTITUTION OF WASHINGTON

Princeton
Princeton University Press
1926

42

"Americans who know the Revolution only through histories of the 'fife and drum' type, in particular, should read this little book," wrote one reviewer of *The American Revolution Considered as a Social Movement* by J. Franklin Jameson. Although the book was published fifty years ago, during the nation's sesquicentennial year of 1926, the advice is still apropos.

As late as 1954 a study lamented that only a few historians had tested the thesis Jameson summarized in a famous sentence: "The stream of revolution, once started, could not be confined within narrow banks, but spread abroad upon the land."

Today, thanks in part to interest stirred by our bicentennial, historians are debating scores of books and monographs written by Jameson's scholar-descendants. Some disagree with him and stress other influences, such as the ideology of the Revolution. Others argue that the social changes were not so sweeping as Jameson suggested, because America was already the freest society in the civilized world. If J. Franklin Jameson were alive today, he would be pleased by this ferment.

Although he published few books, he was a leader in making American history a professional discipline. He was a founder of the American Historical Society and for twenty-six years managing editor of the *American Historical Review*. He was best known in his lifetime for the exploration and description of vast bodies of source materials. His great accomplishment in this field was his leadership of the campaign for the creation of the National Archives.

"He served the needs and interests of generations of scholars far into the future," wrote one of his fellow historians. The words are equally true of the book we are celebrating here.

THOMAS FLEMING
Chairman, American Revolution Round Table

ANNALS OF THE NEW YORK STAGE

BY

GEORGE C. D. ODELL

Professor of Dramatic Literature in Columbia University
Author of Shakespeare from Betterton to Irving

VOLUME ONE
[To 1798]

COLUMBIA UNIVERSITY PRESS
NEW YORK
1927

43 Happy the scholar with a single majestic project to which he is prepared to devote his entire life! George Clinton Densmore Odell was such a scholar; as professor of dramatic literature at Columbia University, he began in 1927 publication of his *Annals of the New York Stage* and was still contentedly at work upon it at the time of his death in 1949, at the age of eighty-three. By then, he had completed the fifteenth of his broad and stout volumes, rounding off, with the profuse chronological particularities of the vaudeville shows of 1894 (including The Four Cohans), a record that had its skimpy origins in the first years of the 18th Century.

On receiving the Gold Medal for Achievement in History in a festive ceremony at the New-York Historical Society in 1942, Odell was described by his fellow scholar Arthur Hobson Quinn as being engaged in "one of the greatest pieces of historical scholarship that the United States has known." But it wasn't a matter of "pieces"— it was simply and grandly a feat, continued in afteryears, with a much diminished felicity and thoroughness of commentary, by our annual series of *Best Plays*.

Odell undertook this superb feat with a sunny confidence in the importance of his subject and, no less, in the importance of his attitude toward his subject. In the best sense of the word, he was an exceedingly old-fashioned historian; his nature was allowed to infuse his labors without the slightest fear of the first person singular.

He wrote at the start: "This history grew out of a great love for the theatre. As boy and as man I have been deeply interested in affairs of the stage, and much of the enjoyment of my life has come from that devotion.... I shall be pleased if my treatment is judged to be both sound and entertaining; with such dual purpose my pen glided happily along."

And in the last volume, the old bachelor-scholar pretends to a distress that we suspect him of being very far from feeling: "I hate to think of the entangled underbrush of names and figures through which I must warily tread my way in writing the history of continuous vaudeville in the Twenty-third Street Theatre. It was a sad day for me and my pen when that species of entertainment came on the scene."

No such thing—only death could stay a hand so eager to pursue its chosen task forever.

BRENDAN GILL
Drama Critic, "The New Yorker"

THE COLONIAL MIND

1620–1800

BY

VERNON LOUIS PARRINGTON

PROFESSOR OF ENGLISH IN THE
UNIVERSITY OF WASHINGTON

NEW YORK

HARCOURT, BRACE AND COMPANY

1927

MAIN CURRENTS IN AMERICAN THOUGHT

AN INTERPRETATION OF AMERICAN LITERATURE
FROM THE BEGINNINGS TO 1920

BY

VERNON LOUIS PARRINGTON

PROFESSOR OF ENGLISH IN THE
UNIVERSITY OF WASHINGTON

VOLUME I ❖ 1620–1800
THE COLONIAL MIND
VOLUME II ❖ 1800–1860
THE ROMANTIC REVOLUTION IN AMERICA
VOLUME III ❖ 1860–1920
THE BEGINNINGS OF CRITICAL REALISM IN AMERICA

44

Main Currents in American Thought by Vernon Louis Parrington, the first two volumes of which (*The Colonial Mind, 1620–1800* and *The Romantic Revolution, 1800–1860*) were published in 1927, the third (*The Beginnings of Critical Realism, 1860–1920*) in 1930, was based on three inspirations. First was the realization that the literature of any people is the outgrowth of the times in which they live, the environment, and their racial peculiarities. The second was the application of the abstract theorizing of political science to the economic realities that underlie and determine them. The third was his realization of American literature as American thought, freeing him from examining the literature merely as belles lettres.

He wrote: "The point of view from which I have endeavored to evaluate the materials is liberal rather than conservative, Jeffersonian rather than federalistic; and very likely in my search I found what I went forth to find. . . ."

The most significant of Parrington's many accomplishments was *Main Currents in American Thought*, which occupied much of his professional life and whose first two volumes met a prompt and enthusiastic response—and won the Pulitzer Prize for the most significant contribution to American history during that year.

While it is easy to hail Parrington as a skillful analyst of American literature, one cannot at the University of Washington cease to be reminded of him as an extraordinary teacher who developed a notable series of lectures in his field of English and American literature and who attracted a wide array of students (from the deadly serious to the casually curious).

Born in Illinois, Parrington received his A.B. at Harvard and his M.A. at the College of Emporia. Subsequently, he studied in London and Paris. He was assistant professor, then professor, of English and American literature at the University of Washington from 1908 until his death in 1929, after serving as an instructor at Emporia in 1893–97 and at Oklahoma, 1897–1908.

MARION A. MILCZEWSKI
Director of Libraries, University of Washington, Seattle

DICTIONARY OF AMERICAN BIOGRAPHY

UNDER THE AUSPICES OF THE
AMERICAN COUNCIL OF LEARNED SOCIETIES

EDITED BY
ALLEN JOHNSON

Abbe — Barrymore
VOLUME I

CHARLES SCRIBNER'S SONS
NEW YORK
1928

45

In 1920, at the first meeting of the newly founded American Council of Learned Societies, Frederick Jackson Turner proposed that the council undertake the preparation of a scholarly reference work of biographies of Americans, on the model of the great British *Dictionary of National Biography*. The work was launched six years later, with funds advanced by Adolph S. Ochs, publisher of *The New York Times*, and the twentieth and last volume of the original edition was published in December 1936. Since then, four supplemental volumes have appeared, bringing the coverage to the end of 1950. Thus far, sixteen thousand and four biographies have been written, by well over three thousand contributors.

While it took many more than these sixteen thousand and four to make America the nation it is today (some of them, indeed, came close to unmaking it), it can be said that the *DAB* presents a gallery of doers and thinkers who made some distinctive mark in their careers and, thus, affected the course of national life. The great among them are dealt with in comprehensive detail, but equally important are the many shorter articles on persons whose contributions have been less well known.

The principles controlling the work were established by a committee of the American Council of Learned Societies, whose report in 1924 included the following: ". . . the articles should be based as largely as possible on original sources; should be the product of fresh work; should eschew rhetoric, sentiment, and coloring matter generally, yet include careful characterization; should be free from the influence of partisan, local, or family prepossessions, striving to the utmost for impartial and objective treatment; should study compression and terseness; and should be written as largely as possible by the persons most specifically qualified. . . ."

The scale of the *DAB*, its universally recognized high scholarly standards, and its readability make it an important contribution to American history in its own right.

Allen Johnson was the first editor. He was succeeded by Dumas Malone, who brought out the last twelve volumes of the original edition. Harris E. Starr, Robert Livingston Schuyler, Edward T. James, and John A. Garraty have been the editors of the supplementary volumes, which continue to be produced at regular intervals.

FREDERICK BURKHARDT
President Emeritus, American Council of Learned Societies;
Chairman, National Commission on Libraries and Information Science

THE PAGEANT OF AMERICA

ANNALS OF AMERICAN SPORT

BY

JOHN ALLEN KROUT

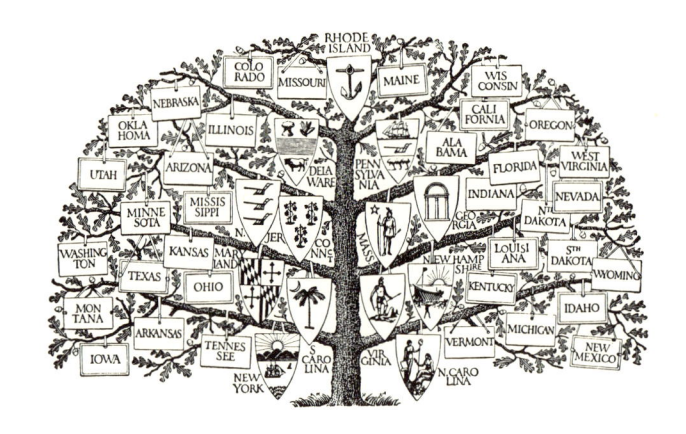

NEW HAVEN · YALE UNIVERSITY PRESS
TORONTO · GLASGOW, BROOK & CO.
LONDON · HUMPHREY MILFORD
OXFORD UNIVERSITY PRESS
1929

46

Ever since the days of the early pioneers, sports have occupied a significant place in American life, yet it was not until the end of this century's third decade that the student, historian, and fan had available a comprehensive survey of this vital subject. The void was filled in 1929 when the Yale University Press published, as the fifteenth and final volume of its "Pageant of America" series, *Annals of American Sport* by John Allen Krout, then assistant professor and now vice-president emeritus at Columbia University.

Krout achieved, between the covers of this single, relatively slim volume, an extensive pictorial history of the wide variety of sports in America from the Colonial period to the late 1920s. Ranging from the skittles of the burghers of New Netherland to contemporary professional football, nearly every sport and champion are included in this book.

The handsome volume is profusely illustrated, featuring hundreds of reproductions of drawings, paintings, photographs, and other pictures to supplement the text. These were culled from a wide variety of sources, and depict many of American sport's most significant people and events (such as a certain prize fight in September of 1927 between two men named Dempsey and Tunney).

Krout's *Annals* was soon recognized as an outstanding contribution, not only to the chronicling of American sport, but also to the study of the historical significance of the nation's pastimes. Applauding the illustrative nature of the book, Allan Nevins, writing in *The Saturday Review of Literature*, observed, "the spirited text which accompanies these pictures is the only good short history of American sport now in existence."

Annals of American Sport remains an important landmark in the continuing examination of our country's life and history. It is also an entertaining book to read.

GENE TUNNEY
Corporation Director;
World's Heavyweight Boxing Champion, 1926–28

MIDDLETOWN

A Study in Contemporary American Culture

by ROBERT S. LYND
and HELEN MERRELL LYND

Foreword by
CLARK WISSLER

NEW YORK
HARCOURT, BRACE AND COMPANY

47

In the early 1920s Robert and Helen Lynd of the Institute for Social and Religious Research at New York City set out to find and study a city which was "as representative as possible of contemporary American life." The results of their work were published in 1929 as the book *Middletown*. The volume examined the selected city from every angle—its habits, culture, religious and community practices, politics, etc.

The book was hailed by sociologists and others as a major study, and remains to this day a monument. (One reviewer said that it "should be engraved upon tablets of stone and buried under a pyramid, so that posterity may know what type of culture prevailed in the Mississippi Valley in the year 1925 A.D.")

The Lynds' "Middletown" was, of course, Muncie, Indiana, called by *Life* magazine "the most interesting small town in the U.S." Their book did not try to flatter local citizens, and some were bothered by their city's being examined so closely and exposed so openly. Most, however, recognized that a true picture had been painted of American life—and willingly co-operated with the Lynds when they returned, a decade later, to do a follow-up survey, published in 1937 as *Middletown in Transition*.

Muncie has nearly doubled in size and has greatly changed since the publication of *Middletown*, nearly half a century ago, but Muncie is still a prime example of the city of America's heartland. It remains typical of our nation's cities in that it shares the problems of larger cities, if perhaps in lesser degree. Yet it is a pleasant and rewarding place in which to work and live.

ROBERT G. CUNNINGHAM
Mayor of Muncie, Indiana

The
Growth of the
American Republic

by

Samuel Eliot Morison
PROFESSOR OF HISTORY IN HARVARD UNIVERSITY

and

Henry Steele Commager
ASSOCIATE PROFESSOR OF HISTORY, NEW YORK UNIVERSITY

New York
OXFORD UNIVERSITY PRESS
LONDON · TORONTO · BOMBAY · MELBOURNE
1930

48

The word "history" is ambiguous. When scholars use the word, they are careful to distinguish its meanings. One may mean the total record, in whatever form, of all which has been done and said in the past, or one may mean the written work of historians themselves. In the former sense, we say that the history of "X" remains to be written; in the latter, we say that a particular book is the history of "X."

For the professional historian interesting problems arise concerning the relation between history, the past itself, and history, the written interpretation of that past by scholars. The layman, though, usually gains his understanding of history not from the primary records of the past, not even from the articles and monographs of specialists, but from the generalist who writes a broad survey of the past.

When, as with Morison and Commager's *Growth of the American Republic*, such a "history" becomes a standard reference, the informed-citizen's guide, and adopted in schools and colleges as a basic text, it has enormous influence on how generations of Americans understand their past.

The late Samuel Eliot Morison, professor of history at Harvard University, was the first Harmsworth Professor at Oxford University, from 1922 to 1925, where he delivered general lectures on the history of the United States. Oxford University Press asked him to make a book of them for the British market. Henry Steele Commager, now one of the most distinguished of our historians, but then a young instructor, suggested the book would make the basis for a fuller and more general history for Americans themselves. Thus began one of the most famous collaborations in American historical writing.

The Growth of the American Republic was first published in 1930, as a single volume, ending its story in 1917. The second edition, carrying the story forward to the year of its publication, 1937, was the first appearance of the familiar two-volume edition. It quickly became the standard history of the United States. By the sixth edition (1969) the authors called upon Prof. William Leuchtenburg of Columbia University to carry on the enterprise.

The Growth of the American Republic may stand as a supreme example of a class of books which have an incalculable influence on the shaping of the American mind, which determine what the general citizen understands history to mean.

JOHN WILLIAM WARD
President, Amherst College

ATLAS
OF THE
HISTORICAL GEOGRAPHY
OF THE
UNITED STATES

BY

CHARLES O. PAULLIN
Carnegie Institution of Washington

Edited by

JOHN K. WRIGHT
Librarian, American Geographical Society of New York

PUBLISHED JOINTLY BY
CARNEGIE INSTITUTION OF WASHINGTON
AND THE
AMERICAN GEOGRAPHICAL SOCIETY OF NEW YORK
1932

49

Conceived by the fertile mind of that historian's historian, John Franklin Jameson, and brought into existence, over a period of two decades, by the labors of more than two score scholars, the *Atlas of the Historical Geography of the United States* is "the first major historical atlas of the United States and probably the most comprehensive work of its kind that has been published for any country."

Although it includes fine reproductions of early maps depicting the existence of a North American continent, "its aim is to illustrate cartographically, in manageable compass, and yet with considerable detail, essential facts of geography and history that condition and explain the development of the United States." To this end the six hundred and eighty-eight maps on one hundred and sixty-six plates, accompanied by one hundred and forty-nine pages of text, present an historical perspective of our explorations, settlement, economy and commerce, and political, social, educational, and religious characteristics.

Jameson, professor of history at Brown and Chicago until 1905, director of the Department of Historical Research of the Carnegie Institution until 1928, and then, during the eighth decade of his life, chief of the Division of Manuscripts at the Library of Congress, first proposed the plan of the *Atlas* in 1903. Until 1927 he closely supervised its progress, choosing the collaborators and deciding on the maps to be included.

Charles Oscar Paullin, Ph.D. from Chicago in Jameson's time and, from 1912 on, a member of the Department of Historical Research, was responsible for the actual preparation of the *Atlas* during this period.

In 1929 an arrangement was made with the American Geographical Society of New York to assume the task of final graphic layout, editing, and publishing under the leadership of John K. Wright, librarian of the society. Some changes in format were made and somewhat over one hundred maps and their accompanying text were added or modified in this final process.

Immediately upon publication, the *Atlas* was hailed as one of the great works of American scholarship—in the words of one reviewer, "quite beyond praise"—and the following year Doctor Paullin received the Loubat Prize for his achievement.

GUSTAVE A. HARRER
Director, University of Florida Libraries

History of Agriculture in the Southern United States To 1860

BY
LEWIS CECIL GRAY
ASSISTED BY
ESTHER KATHERINE THOMPSON

With an Introductory Note by
HENRY CHARLES TAYLOR

VOLUME I

PUBLISHED BY THE CARNEGIE INSTITUTION OF WASHINGTON
WASHINGTON 1933

50

This two-volume set, a companion work to the *History of Agriculture in the Northern United States, 1620–1860* by Bidwell and Falconer, published eight years earlier, is one of the major milestones in American agricultural literature. The author, a professional historian and economist, worked for fourteen years in preparing this very readable, yet comprehensive, treatise.

In the first volume, Part I begins by discussing native agriculture in the South Atlantic region before the arrival of the English, and is followed by a description of the development of agriculture during the Colonial period in Virginia, Maryland, the lower Mississippi valley, the Gulf coastal plains, Georgia, and Florida.

Part II is devoted to the importance of various agricultural industries, with emphasis on such staples as tobacco, rice, and the indigo plant (the latter having been successfully introduced in 1743 by Eliza Lucas); also discussed is the production of hay, animal products, Indian corn, wheat, and other grains.

Parts III and IV deal with the institutional and economic development in the South. The author, with a unique unemotional objectivity, portrays the ante-bellum plantation system as one for managing labor: "a capitalistic type of agricultural organization in which a considerable number of unfree laborers were employed under unified direction and control in the production of a staple crop." He also points out that a majority of Southern people lived on small farms and worked with their own hands.

The second volume covers the period of transition from a Colonial to a national economy, from the American Revolution to the Civil War. It examines the development of the national economy, agricultural industries, and the post-Colonial methods of husbandry.

With its rich statistical information, extensive footnotes, in-depth bibliography, numerous maps, charts, tables, and detailed index, this scholarly work continues to be an essential source of information for researchers of agricultural history in the ante-bellum South.

RICHARD A. FARLEY
Director, National Agricultural Library

A HISTORY OF AMERICAN LIFE
Volume X

THE RISE OF THE CITY
1878-1898

BY
ARTHUR MEIER SCHLESINGER
PROFESSOR OF HISTORY, HARVARD UNIVERSITY

New York
THE MACMILLAN COMPANY
1933

51

That 1776 Colonial America was rural; that 1976 America is urban—these are commonplaces. Yet we sometimes forget the enormity of the contrast. At the time of the Revolution the population was about three million; the largest city had some thirty thousand people; the urban population was some five percent of the total; nineteen of each twenty people lived on a farm. In 1976 the population exceeds two hundred and ten million; four of each five people live in a metropolitan or urban complex.

Arthur Meier Schlesinger Sr.'s *The Rise of the City, 1878-1898* was and remains a seminal work. Indeed, the entire thirteen-volume series "A History of American Life," of which Professor Schlesinger and Dixon Ryan Fox were editors, is seminal, for each volume was a departure from the accepted political-history norm. Professor Schlesinger commented of the series that he "aimed to free American history from its traditional servitude to party struggles, war and diplomacy, and to show that it properly included all the various interests of the people."

If not the sole father of urban history, Professor Schlesinger does have claim to a major share of paternity. In a recent bibliographic listing of volumes on urban history, the total being twenty-eight, the decades of publication were: 1890s—1; 1930s—1; 1940s—1; 1950s—7; 1960s—16; 1970s—2.

Early on, then, Professor Schlesinger perceived and wrote, "The American city has not yet been studied generically nor do there exist any adequate social histories of particular cities."

When his book appeared in 1933 there was much acclaim by reviewers, and that acclaim has persisted in historiographical and bibliographic commentaries. It is true that of the fourteen chapters only two are specifically about the city, but Professor Schlesinger was a social historian, and, as examples, his chapters on "The American Woman," "The Educational Revival," and "The Changing Church" very much relate to the theme.

Mr. Schlesinger once commented to me that anyone who pretended to an interest in American history should read *Uncle Tom's Cabin* at least each five years. It would do no one with a historical interest harm should he or she read *The Rise of the American City, 1878-1898* quinquennially.

This book, for its intrinsic merits and for its representation of the series "A History of American Life," very much belongs among our "76 United Statesiana."

RICHARD W. COUPER
President and Chief Executive Officer,
New York Public Library

THE TERRITORIAL PAPERS OF THE UNITED STATES

Compiled and edited by
Clarence Edwin Carter

VOLUME I

General

PRELIMINARY PRINTING

UNITED STATES
GOVERNMENT PRINTING OFFICE
WASHINGTON : 1934

For sale by the Superintendent of Documents Washington, D.C. - - - - - - - Price 15 cents

52 On April 9, 1783, news reached America that the articles of peace of the Treaty of Paris had gone into effect, and on the same day James Wilson introduced a motion in Congress to appoint a committee to investigate the "measures proper to be taken with respect to the Western Country." With peace, the years of deliberation over how to administer the Western lands ended, and the time for action began.

The history of the world's greatest experiment in planned, systematic, and peaceful growth of republicanism followed. The records of that experiment are contained in the records of the thirty territories, created between 1787 and 1912, that were eventually admitted as equal partners with the states that preceded them.

Compilation and publication of the records of this remarkable political and social innovation began in June 1931 with the appointment of Clarence E. Carter as editor of *The Territorial Papers of the United States*. The work began with Volume II, since Doctor Carter intended that Volume I (issued to date only in a paperback "Preliminary Printing") would contain a selection of papers of a general character, pertaining to two or more territories, as well as a general bibliography of source materials for all the territories.

Twenty-eight volumes covering twelve of the territories are now complete, with the latest volume issued under the editorship of John Porter Bloom, successor to Doctor Carter.

With the project's move from the State Department to the National Archives, after the latter's establishment in 1934, and with endorsement by the National Historical Publications Commission, *The Territorial Papers* joins the documentary histories of *The Ratification of the Constitution*, *The First Federal Elections*, and *The First Congress of the United States* as one of the four pillars supporting the study of the formative years of the American system.

FRANK G. BURKE
Executive Director,
National Historical Publications and Records Commission

LIBRARY OF CONGRESS

GUIDE TO THE DIPLOMATIC HISTORY OF THE UNITED STATES, 1775-1921

By

SAMUEL FLAGG BEMIS
FARNAM PROFESSOR OF DIPLOMATIC HISTORY
IN YALE UNIVERSITY

AND

GRACE GARDNER GRIFFIN
EDITOR OF "WRITINGS ON AMERICAN HISTORY"

UNITED STATES
GOVERNMENT PRINTING OFFICE
WASHINGTON : 1935

53

The *Guide to the Diplomatic History of the United States, 1775–1921* by Samuel Flagg Bemis and Grace Gardner Griffin was published in 1935 and reprinted in 1951. Notwithstanding its age, it remains the most complete guide to the diplomatic history of the United States to 1921. It includes references to American and foreign materials, presenting a view of American diplomacy as seen from both sides.

The *Guide* consists of Part I, a bibliography, and Part II, a treatise on the sources available for investigation. There are numerous cross references from Part I to Part II.

The bibliographical section is arranged by chapters covering in minute detail the years of the American Revolution to the peace settlement following World War I; the arrangement within each chapter is by topic. Bibliographies, monographs, dissertations, speeches and lectures, journal articles, official documents, newspapers, and maps are cited and described.

Part II, entitled "Remarks on the Sources," contains a description of the primary sources, both printed and manuscript, of American diplomatic history and an analysis of their comparative value. The printed materials include the records and published papers of the Department of State and of the other executive departments, as well as the legislative and judicial branches of the United States government. The printed sources also include the state papers of foreign governments and the published records of international organizations. A chapter on manuscript sources provides a guide to archival collections in the United States and abroad. There is an author index and a section referencing papers of the Presidents, Secretaries of State, and American and foreign diplomatists.

In focusing on a vast quantity of materials dealing with nearly a century and a half of American foreign relations, Bemis and Griffin's *Guide to the Diplomatic History of the United States, 1775–1921* has both facilitated and encouraged in-depth research toward a fuller awareness of the history of America and America's role in world affairs.

CONRAD P. EATON
Librarian, United States Department of State

A HISTORY OF AMERICAN MAGAZINES
1741-1850

BY

FRANK LUTHER MOTT

DIRECTOR OF THE SCHOOL OF JOURNALISM
UNIVERSITY OF IOWA

ILLUSTRATED

D. APPLETON AND COMPANY
NEW YORK   LONDON
1930

54

The trouble with calling books classics is that too many people think "classic" is a code-word for "crashing bore." It is therefore important to say at once that Frank Luther Mott's five-volume *A History of American Magazines* is that all-too-rare thing, a lively, readable, eminently un-boring classic.

Anyone who doubts this claim need only browse through the *History*'s listings of long-departed magazines—journals whose titles still ring in the ear and beguile the imagination: the *Panoplist*, *Arcturus*, the *Hesperian*, the *Christian Parlor Magazine*, the *Analectic*, the *Bibelot*, the *Harbinger*. They don't coin titles like that any more. (Though they do "recycle" them: *The Rolling Stone* and *Galaxy* were two 19th Century magazines quite unrelated to their famous present-day namesakes.)

But Mott's *History* (which covers the years from 1741 to 1930) is of course much more than a laundry list of quaint magazine titles; it also not only gives the facts about various publications, it *evokes* them. Thus, Mott holds a mirror up to an entire era when, in discussing *Godey's Lady's Book* (a popular 19th Century periodical) he cites editor Louis A. Godey's response to a reader who has anxiously inquired on which side of the carriage a gentleman should sit. On the left side, replies the irrepressible Godey, for is not this the side "nearest the lady's heart?"

In addition to listing many hundreds of magazines and giving lively summary accounts of key periodicals, Mott sets up subject headings—among them Women's Rights, Morals and the Theater, Acrimonious Weeklies (!), Art Criticism, and Best Sellers—and shows tellingly how the journals of each period dealt with these topics. These compact surveys of changing attitudes make good general reading, and are of course invaluable to social historians and students of journalism.

The first volume of Mott's *History* was issued by Appleton in 1930, the fifth and last by Harvard University Press in 1968. Doctor Mott was born in 1886 in What Cheer (sic!), Iowa. He was for many years professor of journalism at Iowa University and later dean of the University of Missouri School of Journalism. He died in 1964.

His major work, *A History of American Magazines*, remains the pre-eminent study in the field.

NORMAN COUSINS
Editor, "Saturday Review"

THE AMERICAN
AND HIS FOOD

A History of Food Habits in the United States

By

RICHARD OSBORN CUMMINGS

Assistant Professor of History, Lawrence College

THE UNIVERSITY OF CHICAGO PRESS
CHICAGO · ILLINOIS

55

The American and His Food filled a gap in historical knowledge by placing the American diet in its social, technological, agricultural, and medical settings. The book is concise, clear, and vigorous. It is an interesting and excellent demonstration of the historical discipline as practiced by a young historian, with footnotes on almost every page, a dozen illustrations, fifteen appendices, and an index.

The first edition of November 1940 was followed in ten months by a second, in quick response to recommendations of the National Nutrition Conference for Defense in May 1941. The latter is available as a 1970 reprint.

The second edition is divided chronologically, 1789-1941, into five periods. The period 1789-1840 was characterized by the universality of salt pork and corn, and the lack of milk, fresh fruit, and leafy vegetables. After 1830 modest dietary reform began; for example, Graham and unbolted flour. After 1840 technological developments in rail and ocean transport, mechanical refrigeration, cans, and bottles brought fruits, vegetables, milk, and beef to the moderately prosperous.

The years 1881-1916 saw a fight against germs, through containers, milk and water inspections, and controls on preservative chemicals. Improvements in meat transport, slaughtering, and preparation occurred. Nutritional losses resulting from over-refining of sugars and intensively advertised cereals paralleled the emergent "scientific" approach to eating.

Increasingly sophisticated economic organization and nutritional science came after World War I. Grower organizations became influential, and cafeterias simplified food-distribution patterns. The depression years saw federal, state, local, and research agencies zeroing in upon quality and quantity of food, with money, promotion of vitamins, and pure-food laws.

This work was written before cellular and molecular studies took central stage. However, all but two of the essential vitamins had been discovered by 1941.

With intrinsic values of style and content this book combines enduring scholarly quality.

DONALD C. DAVIDSON
University Librarian, University of California, Santa Barbara

DICTIONARY OF AMERICAN HISTORY

JAMES TRUSLOW ADAMS
Editor in Chief

R. V. COLEMAN
Managing Editor

VOLUME I

NEW YORK
CHARLES SCRIBNER'S SONS
1940

56

To build a sense of identity, settlement, and culture may require three hundred years. By 1940 this land had gained that maturity, and United States presence in World War II signified its emergence to international stature. The development had been unsteady, interrupted as it was by the War for Independence, a Civil War of epic proportions, the extraordinary challenges of a frontier extending between two oceans, agonizing adjustments with Indian natives, the Spanish-Mexican accommodation, immigration waves, and cataclysmic technological changes.

The appearance in 1940 of the six-volume *Dictionary of American History* marked, in a sense, the reaching of maturity. Over one thousand historians who contributed to this monumental compilation of sixty-four hundred and twenty-five articles celebrated this event by covering not merely the political and military events, but also the artistic, cultural, economic, geographic, industrial, literary, and social events that defined the American national experience.

The sixth volume is a detailed indexing of the alphabetically ordered topical, signed articles, which include brief bibliographies, and synthesizing "covering articles." The *Atlas of American History* (1943) is a valued companion.

Scribner formed a strong team to produce the *Dictionary of American History*. E. Graham Platt, Frances B. Gallagher, Marion G. Barnes, and Roger Hart performed the major secretariat work. The distinguished advisory council had seven librarians among its seventeen members who helped plan the entire work.

Associate editors Thomas Robson Hay and Ralph Foster Weld aided managing editor R. V. Coleman, an historian from Kansas who had joined Charles Scribner's Sons in 1911, when he was twenty-six years old. The editor-in-chief of this five-year enterprise was James Truslow Adams of Brooklyn, and later Connecticut, who had authored twenty popular American histories and won a Pulitzer Prize.

Henry Steele Commager commented that the *DAH* "covers wide ground . . . it makes no concessions to filiopietism or prejudice, it is accurate, thorough, intelligent, discriminating. It is, in short, indispensable."

Thirty-six years later a revised edition of this American classic has deservedly just appeared.

DAVID C. WEBER
Director, Stanford University Libraries

BIO-BIBLIOGRAPHICAL INDEX OF

MUSICIANS IN THE UNITED STATES OF AMERICA

FROM COLONIAL TIMES

* * *

INDICE BIO-BIBLIOGRAFICO DE

ARTISTAS MUSICALES DE LOS ESTADOS UNIDOS DE AMERICA

DESDE TIEMPOS COLONIALES

* * *

ÍNDICE BIO-BIBLIOGRÁFICO DE

MUSICISTAS DOS ESTADOS UNIDOS DA AMÉRICA

DESDE OS TEMPOS COLONIAIS

Prepared by the
District of Columbia
Historical Records Survey
Division of Community Service Programs
Work Projects Administration

Sponsored by the
Board of Commissioners of the District of Columbia

Co-Sponsors
Pan American Union   Library of Congress

Music Division
Pan American Union
Washington, D.C.
June 1941

57

During the 1930s the United States was engaged in a struggle to regain economic stability. With awakened social consciousness, in a program of government support, agencies were created to provide employment without compromising human dignity, and the Work Progress (later Projects) Administration (WPA), established in 1935, was such an entity. It launched a battery of activities in many areas, and included music among its interests.

In 1936 the Historical Records Survey in the District of Columbia selected the compilation of the *Bio-Bibliographical Index of Musicians in the United States of America from Colonial Times* as part of Federal Project No. 1 of the WPA, its first publication on music and the first part of a projected "Guide to the Study of Music in America." The aim was to list those who have contributed to the history of music in this country and to indicate where information about them can be found.

It is characteristic that no one author is singled out for credit. This was a group project, involving many individuals and several institutions. The Music Division of the Pan American Union, Charles Seeger, chief, sponsored the publication in 1941 and issued a second edition in 1956.

A bibliography of sixty-six reference works, over two-thirds of which have no indices in themselves, precedes the body of the *Index*. The earliest citation dates from 1846; the latest is 1938. (Twelve titles were added in the second edition, to reflect further publications, but these are not coded into the *Index*.)

For each name every effort was made to establish the correct form, to give dates, to indicate foreign-born musicians and country of origin, to describe the individual's activity as concisely as possible, and finally to refer to the entries in the bibliography for more extensive information.

An appendix of over two hundred entries lists special studies, biographies, and autobiographies of individuals mentioned in the *Index*.

Compared with bibliographic works of recent years, the *Index* may appear too simple, lacking in sophistication. The value of this modestly conceived and executed tool, however, is undiminished, as evidenced by its current availability in two reprint editions.

Harold Spivacke, former chief, Division of Music, Library of Congress, has called it "an historical document which summarizes the total human effort expended in the development of the American musical scene."

CLARA STEUERMANN
President, Music Library Association

American Renaissance

ART AND EXPRESSION

IN THE AGE OF EMERSON AND WHITMAN

⇶ ⇷

F. O. MATTHIESSEN

LONDON   TORONTO
OXFORD UNIVERSITY PRESS
NEW YORK

58

Some books are important for what they say and some are important for what they are. F. O. Matthiessen's *American Renaissance* is both and, as such, is represented most appropriately in this American bicentennial exhibit. It is clear that a book need not be a best seller to take an honored place in American letters. From 1941 through 1970 Matthiessen's work sold but thirty thousand copies, a respectable sale (and one still continuing, as do those of most classics), but hardly spectacular.

Subtitling his book "Art and Expression in the Age of Emerson and Whitman," Matthiessen certified for those living in the second half of America's second century that by the end of the first century the new land had produced a literature of the first rank. In this study of the art of Emerson, Thoreau, Whitman, Hawthorne, and Melville, Matthiessen demonstrates that the main current of these five American thinkers and artists was that "The one common denominator of my five writers, uniting even Hawthorne and Whitman, was their devotion to possibilities of democracy."

The book is an outstanding monument of clear and sensitive scholarship based on a humane, vigorous perception of the best in American life. What it said was, and continues to be, important.

Matthiessen provides the insights to the works of the five grand masters of American letters which are possible only through the eyes of "christian socialist." The humanity of his scholarship, as well as its care, continues to impress the current reader, while the political thought, controversial thirty years ago, has proved to be the moderate position on our native ground. What it is is one of those rare intellectual achievements which profoundly moved a whole generation of scholars.

Since its publication in 1941, those who seriously study the literature of this country have continued to testify to the profound impact *American Renaissance* has had on their thought and scholarship, and in so doing to the teachers of American literature it has affected all of us educated in the United States in the last thirty-five years.

HUGH C. ATKINSON
University Librarian, University of Illinois

THE GROWTH OF
AMERICAN THOUGHT

By

MERLE CURTI

Professor of History, University of Wisconsin

ILLUSTRATED

HARPER & BROTHERS PUBLISHERS
NEW YORK AND LONDON

59

This pioneer study of American intellectual development was hailed in the *American Historical Review* as "a major event in American historiography." The author, professor of history at the University of Wisconsin, described his work as "not a history of American thought but a social history . . . and to some extent a socioeconomic history of American thought," relating the state of knowledge, the popular speculations concerning the unknown, the values cherished, and the institutions of research and education to the contemporary social setting.

In scope the work covers the entire period from Colonial times to the eve of World War II. In treatment the author departs from strict chronology to follow the successive social attitudes characteristic of periods of American history: I. The American Adaptation of the European Heritage; II. The Growth of Americanism; III. Patrician Leadership; IV. Democratic Upheaval; V. Triumph of Nationalism in Social and Political Thought; VI. The Assertion of Individualism in a Corporate Age of Applied Science; VII. Optimism Encounters Diversion, Criticism, and Contraction.

Freely utilizing monographic literature, the writer draws selectively also from such sources as theological and scientific treatises, autobiographies, diaries, letters, reports, and popular literature.

The author concludes the introduction with the hope that his work "may help some readers to achieve a fuller appreciation of our country's past."

In American intellectual history Merle Curti ranks with Carl L. Becker, Ralph H. Gabriel, and Richard Hofstadter. The first edition of *The Growth of American Thought* won for the author the Pulitzer Prize for the most significant work of American history published in 1943. New editions (1951, 1964) confirmed his reputation and assured him a place of distinction beside V. L. Parrington, whose *Main Currents in American Thought* received the Pulitzer Prize for 1927, and Perry Miller, whose posthumous book *The Life of the Mind in America* took the Pulitzer Prize for 1965.

STANLEY MCELDERRY
Director, University of Chicago Library

A TREASURY OF
AMERICAN
FOLKLORE

STORIES, BALLADS, AND
TRADITIONS OF THE PEOPLE

Edited by
B. A. BOTKIN

In Charge of The Archive of American Folk Song of the Library of Congress

with a Foreword by
CARL SANDBURG

CROWN PUBLISHERS
NEW YORK

60

No American scholar or editor would have the temerity to claim he had compiled a work which in a single volume tapped the American imagination and expressed the whole range of American social attitudes. Nor did Benjamin A. Botkin make this claim for *A Treasury of American Folklore* before or after the first (in 1944) of its more than twenty printings. Yet this nine hundred and thirty-two page volume, with its almost infinite variety of folk stories, legends, tall tales, jokes, proverbs, rhymes, songs, and ballads, comes as close to being a definitive compilation of American expressive culture as any anthology ever will.

Though its editor had impeccable academic credentials (he was president of the American Folklore Society and head of the Folk Music Section of the Library of Congress) and the book was to become the best-known and most widely read work on American folklore, it was not received universally with acclaim. A few academic folklorists saw this volume, and the regional treasuries which followed, as travesties —in the misuse of the term "folklore"—noting the inclusion of materials from literary, rather than exclusively oral, sources and the omission of various genres.

As a close reading of it reveals, Botkin's introduction (later referred to by Herbert Halpert, in his presidential address to the American Folklore Society in 1955, as "one of the best introductions to folklore that I know") states his reasons for his omissions and explains his inclusions. Botkin's approach was "broadly literary and social rather than strictly folkloristic," and he was one of the earliest scholars to explore the relationships in American expressive culture between folklore, popular culture, and formal literature. His detractors should have taken their ire out on his publishers for having misleadingly called his books "treasuries of folklore." (A number of his severest critics later tried their own hands at compiling similar works, falling considerably short of his success—both in scope and in public appreciation.)

In the final analysis it was Botkin's work, together with that of the equally maligned song collections of John and Alan Lomax, which fired the imagination of the young Americans who populated the post–World War II university folklore classes of both his admirers and detractors, and it is from these ranks that a large number of the present generation of academic folklorists came. More important to the history of American social thought, Botkin and *A Treasury of American Folklore* introduced to millions of readers the vital nature and virile substance of American folk and popular lore.

KENNETH S. GOLDSTEIN
President, American Folklore Society

MEN OF SCIENCE
IN AMERICA

*The Role of Science in the
Growth of Our Country*

BY
BERNARD JAFFE

New York
SIMON AND SCHUSTER
1944

61

American science bears the imprint of a new and growing nation that matured in concert with the industrial revolution. From its earliest days America fostered the natural sciences, as its people moved inland to explore, inventory, and use the land and natural resources over which they gained hegemony. The abstract sciences lagged the European experience, for want of nurture by a society that gave priority to ingenuity, inventiveness, technology, and industry. "The spirit of America," said de Tocqueville, "is averse to general ideas and does not seek theoretical discoveries."

Abstract sciences began to flourish in America in the late-19th Century, as major business enterprises in basic industries sought to sustain their profits through research and American graduate education provided an impetus for faculty research. This quickened the pace of scientific discovery and gave greater emphasis to theoretical science.

America reached its stride beginning with World War II and the advent of "big science" which requires massive funding that only the rich and developed nations can afford.

This is the web of Bernard Jaffe's *Men of Science in America*. His theme is expressed through the work and lives of twenty great scientists born or at work in America from the 17th Century onwards.

From Jaffe's accounts of the scientists' lives and the state of scientific development through the years, there emerges a vision of the American experience in science —slowly developing but unfettered by authoritarianism in its early years, ultimately eclectic, and capable in any field.

The experience is one of government impetus without a unified national science policy during most of its history, of the encouragement of science on behalf of commercial and national interests, of scientists interested in social, economic, and political issues, but generally unable to influence the exploitation of science. It shows an American society that, after all, requires scientific advances.

RUSSELL SHANK
Director of Libraries, Smithsonian Institution

Ordeal of the Union

VOLUME I... | *FRUITS OF MANIFEST DESTINY* 1847·1852

by ALLAN NEVINS

"Political history, to be intelligible and just, must be based on social history in its largest sense"
LETTERS OF JOHN RICHARD GREEN

New York · CHARLES SCRIBNER'S SONS · *London*
1947

62

Allan Nevins, who used and supported libraries with the same intensity he displayed writing and teaching history, spoke towards the end of his life of the librarian's duty not only to know and distribute books, but "to buy them enthusiastically, read them enthusiastically, and insofar as the books deserve it, talk about them enthusiastically."

His own historical series called "Ordeal of the Union" fully deserves enthusiastic acclaim and has, in fact, been hailed by historians and students of history for its breadth of scope, wealth and balance of fact, and quality of writing. By and large, these characteristics are hallmarks of all of Nevins' work, produced as he pursued with uncommon energy not only an understanding of the past, but a better comprehension of the present.

His long career at Columbia and, following retirement from teaching, at the Huntington Library was one of awesome productivity. More than fifty books came from his typewriter, he edited nearly seventy-five others, and he wrote hundreds of articles and reviews—all of this while teaching a full schedule, supervising doctoral candidates, and protecting and promoting development of resources for use by future generations of historians.

The first four volumes of "Ordeal of the Union," covering the period 1847–61, describe with care and feeling a country in transition and chronicle the development of the issues and the emergence of the man that were to bring, first, conflict and, then, direction to our nation. The four final volumes (the last two of which were published after Nevins' death in 1971) focus on the war itself.

Volumes I and II (1947) bore *Ordeal of the Union* as their main title; Volumes III and IV (1950) had *The Emergence of Lincoln* as main-title element; and Volumes V through VIII (1959–71) were designated *The War for the Union*.

Throughout, economic, social, intellectual, and political events are carefully considered and effectively linked. Nevins used the conceptual tools of the social sciences, but he viewed history fundamentally as a dramatic story, and sought to keep the techniques subservient to the art.

In a recent reminiscence, Ray Allen Billington notes the depth of Nevins' feelings about his subject, and by way of illustration quotes Nevins himself, who wrote, "written history has changed the destiny of nations, and without it there can be neither true liberty nor true patriotism." For Nevins, the importance of historical scholarship was beyond question, because the only acceptable result, accurate and precisely written history, was essential to citizenship.

WARREN J. HAAS
Vice-President and University Librarian, Columbia University

History and Bibliography of American Newspapers

1690-1820

BY

CLARENCE S. BRIGHAM

VOLUME ONE

AMERICAN ANTIQUARIAN SOCIETY
WORCESTER, MASSACHUSETTS
1947

63

When Clarence Saunders Brigham's *History and Bibliography of American Newspapers, 1690–1820* was published in 1947 it was described by Lawrence C. Wroth, in the *New York Herald Tribune*, as having the unique distinction of being "a classic production of its kind" *before* it was printed. It deserved this reputation, because the work known to scholars as "Brigham's American Newspapers" began its appearance in the *Proceedings of the American Antiquarian Society* in 1913, and was completed there in 1927.

A fifty-page supplement appeared in April 1961, and the American Antiquarian Society and Barre Publishers in 1972 brought out *Chronological Tables of American Newspapers, 1690–1820*, which was based on the Brigham two-volume study.

The original work and supplementary efforts, thus, constitute a work of scholarship commenced sixty-five years ago.

More than two thousand different newspapers were printed in America from 1690 to 1820. They are a mine of historical reference material, numbering by some estimates more than seven hundred thousand separate documents, deposited in five hundred public libraries and one hundred and twenty-five private libraries.

To make such a vast reservoir of historical material of use for scholarly inquiry required the sort of orderly enumeration on which Brigham began in 1913. The "Microprint Edition of Early American Newspapers" by Readex Microprint Corporation and the American Antiquarian Society further opened up this treasure to scholars.

A greatly sharpened scholarly perception of the utility of newspapers for purposes of historical research has gone hand in hand with the great improvement in the means of examining the newspapers. Brigham's two-volume bibliography, with its orderly enumeration of American newspapers, state by state, and city by city, with relevant publishing data, increased scholarly interest at the same time that it diminished the difficulty of using newspapers.

Brigham sensed that historians of the future would pay more attention to newspapers than those of the past had paid to them. He prophesied that they would; and his book made his prophecy self-fulfilling.

JAMES RUSSELL WIGGINS
*Editor and Publisher, "The Ellsworth (Maine) American";
President, American Antiquarian Society*

The American Political Tradition

And the Men Who Made It

BY

RICHARD HOFSTADTER

NEW YORK *Alfred A. Knopf* 1948

64

Published on the eve of the election of 1948, this second in a series of influential books placed the author in the forefront of students of United States history. Broad in coverage, sophisticated in judgment, and graceful in style, the volume offered a witty, caustic, and daring challenge to the progressive interpretation of the past—embodied in the works of Charles A. Beard, Carl L. Becker, and Vernon L. Parrington—with its emphasis on conflict between the "people" and the "interests."

Using previously demonstrated skills as a historian of ideas and keen biographical insights, Hofstadter argued that American leaders had always agreed on fundamentals—the rights of property, the value of free enterprise, and the virtue of economic individualism. The result was a landmark in the new political history and, for some, in consensus history, though the author disliked and, indeed, eluded such historiographical categorizations.

The chapter titles suggest the scope and flavor: "The Founding Fathers: An Age of Realism"; "Thomas Jefferson: The Aristocrat as Democrat"; "Andrew Jackson and the Rise of Liberal Capitalism"; "John C. Calhoun: The Marx of the Master Class"; "Abraham Lincoln and the Self-Made Myth"; "Wendell Phillips: The Patrician as Agitator"; "The Spoilsmen: An Age of Cynicism"; "William Jennings Bryan: The Democrat as Revivalist"; "Theodore Roosevelt: The Conservative as Progressive"; "Woodrow Wilson: The Conservative as Liberal"; "Herbert Hoover and the Crisis of American Individualism"; "Franklin D. Roosevelt: The Patrician as Opportunist."

Reprinted eleven times, *The American Political Tradition* was widely used in college courses for over two decades. A twenty-fifth anniversary edition appeared in 1973, with an introductory evaluation by Christopher Lasch. The volume foreshadowed themes of later books, two of which won Pulitzer Prizes.

In 1970, a few months before Hofstadter was to become president of the Organization of American Historians, his extraordinarily rich and productive career was, at the age of fifty-four, prematurely terminated by leukemia.

RICHARD W. LEOPOLD
President, Organization of American Historians

THE INDEX OF AMERICAN DESIGN

ERWIN O. CHRISTENSEN

INTRODUCTION BY HOLGER CAHILL

THE MACMILLAN COMPANY: NEW YORK

NATIONAL GALLERY OF ART
SMITHSONIAN INSTITUTION, WASHINGTON, D. C.

1950

65

"The true character of Americans is mirrored in their homes," said the perceptive French émigré Moreau de St. Méry as he toured America in the 1790s. His observation suggests that a reflection of the kind of people who were uprooted from the old world and transplanted in the new—the hopes and ideal that inspired them, the creative skills and unconscious artistry that sustained them—could be viewed best in the ephemeral, functional objects they made.

"Art begins in the irresponsible imaginations of the people," the English stylist George Moore once said. Spurning the embellishments and lavishness of the grand style of the refined arts, Americans tended to simplify ornament and emphasize line and proportion in their craftsmanship, when adapting patterns from abroad to their needs.

In *The Index of American Design*, Erwin Ottomar Christensen (1890–1975) assembled a rich, colorful, and representative collection of America's arts of use and necessity, the product of "scholarship with brush and paint": here are ship's figureheads and cigar-store Indians, Shaker furniture and Conestoga wagons, glassware and pottery, woven coverlets and patchwork quilts, commercial shop signs and decorative ironwork, party clothes and children's toys—the work of untrained designers but highly skilled craftsmen.

It took the economic depression of the 1930s to launch the ambitious project of recording pictorially (mostly in meticulous watercolors, but including some photographs) the "articles in daily use in this country from early colonial times to the close of the nineteenth century." Between 1935 and 1939 numerous unemployed artists and craftsmen were hired by the Federal Art Project of the WPA program to record and research a cultural stockpile of some fifteen thousand objects, known as the Index of American Design and housed in the National Gallery of Art in Washington.

Through a carefully contrived balance between text and three hundred and seventy-eight pictures selected from this archive, Christensen produced the first extensive, orderly, and accurate published account of the American arts used for daily living. In his panoramic anthology can be found, in addition to pure entertainment, a better understanding of the ever-flowing, ever-changing springs of invention in American craftsmen.

WENDELL GARRETT
Editor and Publisher, "The Magazine Antiques"

by

MARSHALL B. DAVIDSON

Life *in* America

IN TWO VOLUMES: VOL. I

Published in Association with the Metropolitan Museum of Art

HOUGHTON MIFFLIN COMPANY BOSTON

The Riverside Press Cambridge

1951

"In the crowded world of American publishing there appears but seldom a work that takes a distinct step forward or that merits the weary copywriter's adjective "unique." Such a book, when it first appeared in 1951, was *Life in America* by Marshall B. Davidson, at that time editor of publications at the Metropolitan Museum of Art and previously associate curator of that institution's American Wing. Out of great erudition and long search through the vast but disorganized resources of American iconography—paintings, drawings, sketches, photographs, old wood-block illustrations, and the like—he assembled a two-volume social, cultural, economic, and philosophical history of this country. Politics and war are not absent, either, but in proper perspective; they do not dominate.

What makes it all a landmark is Davidson's pioneer work in integrating a rich and interesting text, full of quotations from the times, with a thitherto unmatched collection of contemporary illustration.

Pictures and text move along together, arm in arm, so to speak, each supporting the other, each enhancing the other. Not for Davidson the separate signatures of illustrations here and there, not for him the busy flipping back and forth of pages to find Fig. 97 or Plate XXIV or whatever is being discussed in the text. There it is, before you. If this seems a less than revolutionary idea now, twenty-five years after *Life in America* first came out, listen to what Bernard De Voto wrote then in his *New York Herald Tribune* review:

"*Life in America* is an almost unbelievably successful attempt to increase understanding of our past by employing the resources of graphic visualization. It is a tremendous feat both of historical creation and of printing. It consists of a quarter of a million words of letterpress and twelve hundred illustrations fused together in an account of our historical experience. The fusion has to be insisted upon, for it is the point of the endeavor.... It is not ... a 'picture book' .... It is history—historical exposition, interpretation, and comment—which uses pictures to extend and enhance historical realization."

Since *Life in America* appeared, the floodgates of illustrated history have opened wide, with results running from the superficial to the intensely valuable. Even the most austere academic historians, who once thought illustration a trifling matter, have revised their ideas. (You will now find—imagine!—pictures in the *American Historical Review*.) And there at the head of the parade, as fresh and readable as ever, is Davidson's wonderful work.

OLIVER JENSEN
Senior Editor, "American Heritage: The Magazine of History"

The Uprooted

*The Epic Story of the
Great Migrations that Made
the American People*

BY OSCAR HANDLIN

AN ATLANTIC MONTHLY PRESS BOOK
LITTLE, BROWN AND COMPANY · BOSTON
1951

67

The epic story of the uprooting of tens of millions of rural people, and their efforts to begin again in a new land, is more than just national history, it is part of most of our family histories. We stand on the shoulders of those who left the small farms of Europe for the ghettos of New York, Boston, and Chicago.

The story is a tragic one, for many died in steerage and many more failed to find the fabled "opportunity" of America. Instead, they found disease, violence, discrimination, and injustice.

Prof. Oscar Handlin of Harvard writes with authority, as his research began with the writing of his dissertation in 1940, a study on the acculturation of Boston immigrants. This is not a dull, scholarly compilation, however, nor is it a retelling of the popular myth. It is a poignant, appealing, and highly personal account of individual and family experiences drawn from newspapers, diaries, and history books by a scholar who places greater emphasis on the effects of events on people than on the events themselves. It is told in straightforward prose that will appeal to all Americans.

Oscar Handlin has been a teacher of history at Harvard since 1939. His writings include not only the Pulitzer Prize–winning *The Uprooted*, but also, among others, *This Was America* (1949), *The American People in the Twentieth Century* (1954), *Race and Nationality in American Life* (1956), and *The Wealth of the American People* (1975). He is the recipient of numerous honorary degrees from institutions ranging from Maine to Michigan, and he takes special pride in his appointment as a trustee of the New York Public Library.

RICHARD W. BOSS
University Librarian, Princeton University

Origins of the
New South
1877-1913

BY C. VANN WOODWARD

LOUISIANA STATE UNIVERSITY PRESS
THE LITTLEFIELD FUND FOR SOUTHERN
HISTORY OF THE UNIVERSITY OF TEXAS
1951

A HISTORY
OF
THE SOUTH

Volume IX

EDITORS

WENDELL HOLMES STEPHENSON
PROFESSOR OF SOUTHERN HISTORY
AT TULANE UNIVERSITY

E. MERTON COULTER
PROFESSOR OF HISTORY AT THE
UNIVERSITY OF GEORGIA

68

C. Vann Woodward is the leading authority on the history of the South since the Civil War and Reconstruction. Two important decisions were necessary, however, before he could undertake the task of writing *Origins of the New South, 1877–1913*. First, the editors of the proposed monumental ten-volume "History of the South" had to determine whether Woodward, then a relatively young and not fully established historian, should be invited to write the book. Second, the prospective author had to be concerned about his qualifications for the work and the difficult task that would face him, for this was a period and subject that scholars had tended to leave to others. A happy determination was made on both sides, and the book that resulted is unusually revealing and authoritative.

The volume is a thoughtful, discerning history of the South from the end of Reconstruction to the Wilson era, a period of traumatic transition. Civil War and Reconstruction led inevitably to confusion, corruption, and decay. New modes of life and association did not come easily. Problems of race and poverty added immeasurably to the difficulties of the South.

The book conveys a sense of sadness and regret, perhaps imagined by a fellow Southerner, about the ineptitude of Southern leaders at the time who, when restored to office, failed to show the way out of gloom and lethargy and mismanagement.

As Woodward shows, the title *Origins of the New South* is somewhat misleading if it tends to suggest an impending era of improvement, modernization, and progress. "New South" was largely a widely publicized slogan of the period, with little basis in fact. The book shows other origins more clearly: those of white supremacy, Colonial economy, cultural deprivation, political manipulation, and "Jim Crow." It was not a happy period.

The book is excellent history and one of the most important about the South.

FRED C. COLE
President, Council on Library Resources

People of Plenty

*Economic Abundance
and the American Character*

By DAVID M. POTTER

THE UNIVERSITY OF CHICAGO PRESS

69

David M. Potter's *People of Plenty* (1954) is a study of the essential nature of the American mind and experience. It ranks in importance with Frederick Jackson Turner's famous frontier theory, making Potter, in the words of Sir Denis Brogan, "one of the truly great interpreters of American history."

Potter examines the nature of American abundance and its effect, as an historical force, on some of America's distinctive ideals, institutions, and social practices, employing the methods of social psychology and cultural anthropology.

He argues that human enterprise and capacity for productive work, quite as much as the profusion of resources, account for the achievements of American society. He analyzes the contradictions between American social mobility and the idea of status (which in other societies has meant an immutable station in the social system, but in America he anticipates a more beneficent form of status, enhancing personal identity and place in the community).

Abundance is conducive to democracy and altered standards of social justice which disincline Americans to class struggle in favor of using "nature's surplus and technology's tricks" to deal with problems of social reform. But Americans have failed to realize, in attempting to export our system to other countries, that it was abundance that broadened the basis of our democracy, not abstract political ideals, and therefore attempts to fulfill the mission of America elsewhere have been largely misunderstood and frustrated.

Potter finds Turner's agrarian theory of settlement oversimplified, recognizes the social influence of advertising not possible in a scarcity economy, and demonstrates how "plenty" affects the rearing of children and the position of women in the United States in ways pervasive in the formation of the American character.

David Morris Potter (1910–71), a Georgian by birth, was graduated from Emory University in 1932, and received his Ph.D. from Yale in 1940. At the time of his death he was Coe Professor of History at Stanford University and president of both the American Historical Association and the Organization of American Historians.

THOMAS R. BUCKMAN
President, The Foundation Center

BIBLIOGRAPHY OF
American Literature

COMPILED BY JACOB BLANCK

for the Bibliographical Society of America

VOLUME ONE
HENRY ADAMS TO DONN BYRNE

NEW HAVEN: *Yale University Press*
London: Geoffrey Cumberlege, Oxford University Press
1955

70

The title page reproduced here opens a volume of four hundred and seventy-four pages that is but the initial one of a projected set of eight or nine of similar scope, whose purpose is to provide a descriptive bibliography of the first editions of some three hundred authors of American literature.

About twenty years of work lay behind this publication; almost twenty more years passed before Volume VI appeared, the last to be issued prior to the death of their creator, Jacob Blanck, in 1974 at the age of sixty-eight. He built so well and carefully that the rest of the volumes will follow in due course.

Blanck's bibliography sets forth descriptions of the first forms of publication—books, pamphlets, leaflets, and broadsides—by a great aggregation of American authors of belles lettres who lived between the beginning of the Federal period and the end of 1930.

Journal and newspaper appearances, unrevised reprints of books, and all translations are left to future bibliographers of individual authors of major consequence, but one cannot anticipate more thorough treatments of the many lesser literati than that afforded by the *Bibliography of American Literature*.

As the result of patient and precise examination of thousands upon thousands of books (the forty-one authors of Volume I alone requires twenty-three hundred and twenty-eight entries), Jacob Blanck has created an imposing bibliographical survey, title by title, of a substantial array of America's writers, major and minor, such as had long been needed and wanted by all persons who are deeply concerned with the publication of our national literature.

       JAMES D. HART
       Director, Bancroft Library;
       Editor, "The Oxford Companion to American Literature"

MILITARY HERITAGE
OF AMERICA

R. Ernest Dupuy
COLONEL, UNITED STATES ARMY, RETIRED

Trevor N. Dupuy
COLONEL, UNITED STATES ARMY

McGRAW-HILL BOOK COMPANY, INC.

New York   Toronto   London

1956

Albert Einstein once wrote, "Peace cannot be kept by force. It can only be achieved by understanding." As we nurture the first generation of Americans who have never experienced the terrors of war, we must strive to instill in them an understanding of the concepts and precepts of war—lest they be forced to experience it. *Military Heritage of America* provides a base for this understanding.

This book explores, with thought, the wars of this nation from the Revolutionary period through the Korean conflict and provides a reader with insight into our martial traditions and heritage. This work is as important to the student of military sciences as is a study of the works of Jomini or Von Clausewitz. This treatise provides the interested citizen with enough knowledge of our military heritage to create in him an understanding and awareness of the American way of war.

Both authors, a father and son, have dedicated their lives to the service of their country in the United States Army. Their efforts as teachers of military sciences and as historians have carved for them a niche in the annals of military history, alongside such names as Von Clausewitz, Churchill, and Eisenhower.

If we are to believe that past is but prologue, then this work is even more valid today than when it was first published, twenty years ago. If we are to leave our children a legacy of peace, then our legacy of war must be understood. This book can help create that understanding.

Mrs. Paul Brown
National President, American Legion Auxiliary

A Monetary History
of the
United States
1867-1960

MILTON FRIEDMAN
ANNA JACOBSON SCHWARTZ

A STUDY BY THE
NATIONAL BUREAU OF ECONOMIC RESEARCH, NEW YORK

PUBLISHED BY
PRINCETON UNIVERSITY PRESS, PRINCETON
1963

72

This work of Milton Friedman and Anna Schwartz is a major and challenging contribution to both the economic history of the United States and to monetary economics. It traces the history of the stock of money and of the institutions responsible for its creation and control over a period of nearly one hundred years, from the close of the Civil War until 1960. It examines the causes determining changes in the stock of money, and it endeavors to trace the effect of such changes on the course of prices and economic activity.

Milton Friedman is recognized the world over as one of the most creative, influential, and controversial economists of the post–World War II period, and as the founder and undisputed leader of the "monetarist school." He has devoted much of his scientific life to establishing the thesis that money plays a predominant role in business fluctuations—at a time when this view was by no means widely accepted.

From this perspective, special significance attaches to the chapter on the Great Depression. Here the authors vigorously set out the thesis that a major cause of the length and severity of this contraction—the greatest economic catastrophe of modern history—is to be found in the unprecedented decline in the stock of money by about one-third between 1929 and 1933. It is argued that the decline can be attributed to a series of gross mistakes on the part of the Federal Reserve.

Anna Schwartz is a member of the staff of the National Bureau of Economic Research, a venerable organization founded by Wesley C. Mitchell in 1920, which has played a central role in advancing our understanding of the business cycle, through the systematic collection and analysis of an impressive array of economic time series. This book is one of the fruits of that research and is included in the NBER series "Studies in Business Cycles."

FRANCO MODIGLIANI
President, American Economic Association

A TOWER IN BABEL

A History of Broadcasting
in the United States

Volume I—to 1933

ERIK BARNOUW

New York OXFORD UNIVERSITY PRESS 1966

Of the many technological developments which have come about during our history, few—some would say none—have had so profound an effect on the fabric of American life as radio and television. They are now such a part of our daily lives that we occasionally fail to appreciate how relatively new these innovations are. Regular radio broadcasting in the United States began only in 1920, and yet today over ninety-nine percent of all American homes supplied with electricity have at least one radio and television set.

The initial volume of the first truly comprehensive chronicle of the life of the young industry was Erik Barnouw's *A Tower in Babel*, published in 1966, which detailed the rapid growth of broadcasting, from its beginnings to President Franklin D. Roosevelt's first "fireside chat" of 1933.

The second volume of *A History of Broadcasting in the United States* was entitled *The Golden Web* and appeared in 1968. It examined the great national networks, whose growth dominated the next two decades of the life of American broadcasting.

The trilogy was completed in 1970 with the publication of *The Image Empire*, winner the following year of the Bancroft Prize. This volume brought the chronology up to date and focused on the growing international role of America's radio and television.

"A television-radio system," wrote Barnouw, "is like a nervous system. It sorts and distributes information, igniting memories. It can speed or slow the pulse of society. The impulse it transmits can stir the juices of emotion, and can trigger action. As in the case of a central nervous system, aberrations can deeply disturb the body politic. These complex roles lend urgency to the study of television and radio and the forces and mechanisms that guide and control them."

In his examination of American broadcasting from its infancy to its present gigantic stature, Professor Barnouw has provided that study.

VINCENT T. WASILEWSKI
President, National Association of Broadcasters

SYDNEY E. AHLSTROM

A RELIGIOUS HISTORY OF THE AMERICAN PEOPLE

NEW HAVEN AND LONDON: YALE UNIVERSITY PRESS

Published in 1972

To appreciate the scope of Mr. Ahlstrom's achievement, the reader must be sensitive to the promise of his title, *A Religious History of the American People*. Although his book could well qualify as a work of church history, he has set himself four further conditions to make it true *religious* history. He has placed his story in the larger framework of world history, and he bears in mind, throughout, the period's social context. He lists as religious even some secular movements that are based on moral seriousness. Finally, he is wary of any interpretation based on a single or unified "American" tradition which does not do justice to the radical diversity of American religious movements.

In the process he has also given us a masterly summary of the history of individual churches which, if he had so chosen, might have been the foundation of an encyclopedia of American church history. At one point, he observes that to do justice to a certain point could easily produce "a sterile catalogue or a long book." It is a tribute to his powers of organization that his work of more than a thousand pages never seems long, and always maintains a sense of the unity of the whole.

There are two things which prevent these pages from becoming a sterile catalogue. First, he is always in control of the vast amount of material he has synthesized. He lets us know where he feels that an area has not received the attention it deserves from scholars, as in the case of the black churches, or where he disagrees with previous interpretations, as in his high opinion of the work of Jonathan Edwards. Second, his knowledge of American theology and its relationships with world religions has enabled him to help us understand the full intellectual background of the religious development he describes.

In this bicentennial year, as Americans search for the spiritual roots of the traditions which have brought them this far, we are fortunate to have a work of this caliber as an aid in that search.

TERENCE CARDINAL COOKE
Archbishop of New York

THE AMERICANS
THE DEMOCRATIC EXPERIENCE

Daniel J. Boorstin

> "American life is a powerful solvent."
> GEORGE SANTAYANA

Random House | New York

75

This volume finishes a series which Professor Boorstin set out a quarter of a century ago to write; the others are *The Colonial Experience* (1958) and *The National Experience* (1965). The fresh approach which the books reflect is extraordinary, and it is carried out with notable success.

All of the volumes of this trilogy have won prestigious awards: a Bancroft Prize for the first; a Francis Parkman Prize for the second; and a Pulitzer Prize for *The Americans: The Democratic Experience*, following its publication in 1973. In them history is not wars, elections, social conflict, the traumas and triumphs of great movements of opinion, but the more basic things of what it is hard to call—in the period covered by this volume (since the Civil War)—anything but "the democratic experience."

"Democratic" does not refer to politics or to the structure of government, except to a minor degree (lawyers, crime, politics in cities, etc.), but to the developments which concern the lives of all the people directly. Thus, the cattle business, agriculture, railroads, automobiles, invention and technology in all its phases, real-estate developments, the corporate way, merchandising (including packaging, advertising), statistics and accounting, the growth of cities, the impact of immigration have their place. But so do developments in the language, schoolteaching, higher education, religion, oratory, and other matters of the intellect and the feelings.

The impact of all these things, as well as many more, on how the people are leveled or otherwise made—or unmade—in their morals and their sense of community, is stated in broad terms, and without obvious ideological slant. The result is a truly original, exciting, and learned—but fast-flowing and attention-holding—story.

Georgia-born in 1914 and raised in Oklahoma, Daniel J. Boorstin has had a distinguished career as attorney, teacher, author, and administrator, culminating in his appointment in 1975 as twelfth Librarian of Congress. He assumed his position as head of our national library immediately after having served as senior historian of the Smithsonian Institution and director of its National Museum of History and Technology.

LUTHER H. EVANS
Librarian of Congress, 1945–53

Michigan

A Bicentennial History

Bruce Catton

W. W. Norton & Company, Inc.
New York

American Association for State and Local History
Nashville

The first volume to be published (1976) in a bicentennial series "The States and the Nation," intended to include histories of each of the fifty United States of America, as well as the District of Columbia; prepared under sponsorship of the American Association for State and Local History and through support from the National Endowment for the Humanities.

76 I commend those individuals and organizations who have assembled this lasting tribute to the United States bicentennial. I also congratulate Mr. Bruce Catton on his fine literary contribution to the works on the fifty states. *Michigan: A Bicentennial History* is a masterful review of the history of our native state and its role in the growth and the development of our nation.

The series of books on the states reflects the close association between their history and the history of the nation as a whole. While each state can claim its own individual characteristics and unique citizens, their stories are a reflection of the story of America.

This collection is a tribute to the spirit and the strength of the American people. It is their story and the retelling of their proud past. It is also descriptive of the American adventure today.

Mr. Catton says it well: "We live in a time of change, and it has a truly explosive quality coming from the new faith by which men nowadays live—the faith in man's capacity to do anything on earth that he really wants to do."

GERALD R. FORD
President of the United States

Index

Index to the authors, editors, and compilers of the works featured herein, as well as to the writers of the commentaries relating thereto. References are to item numbers.

Abbott, Benjamin Vaughan 17
Ackerman, Page 29
Adams, Henry 21
Adams, James Truslow 56
Agassiz, Louis 15
Ahlstrom, Sydney E. 74
Andrews, John B. 34
Armstrong, Rodney 27
Atkinson, Edward 17
Atkinson, Hugh C. 58

Bancroft, George 10
Barnard, F. A. P. 17
Barnouw, Erik 73
Beard, Charles A. 33
Belknap, Jeremy 1
Bell, Whitfield J., Jr. 3
Bemis, Samuel Flagg 53
Blanck, Jacob 70
Bloom, John Porter 52
Boorstin, Daniel J. 75
Boss, Richard W. 67
Botkin, Benjamin A. 60
Brace, Charles L. 17
Brandeis, Elizabeth 34
Brewer, W. H. 17
Brigham, Clarence Saunders 63
Bristol, Roger Pattrell 27
Broderick, John C. 28
Brooke, Edward W. 17

Brown, Mrs. Paul 71
Bryant, Douglas W. 19
Buchwald, Art 36
Buckman, Thomas R. 69
Budington, William S. 41
Burger, Warren E. 39
Burke, Frank G. 52
Burkhardt, Frederick 45

Carter, Clarence Edwin 52
Catton, Bruce 76
Census, Bureau of the 31
Channing, Edward 23
Christensen, Erwin Ottomar 65
Cole, Fred C. 68
Coleman, R. V. 56
Commager, Henry Steele 48
Commerce and Labor, Department of 31
Commons, John R. 34
Conant, S. S. 17
Cooke, Terence Cardinal 74
Couper, Richard W. 51
Cousins, Norman 54
Cummings, Richard Osborn 55
Cunningham, Robert G. 47
Curti, Merle 59
Cutter, Donald C. 37

Davidson, Donald C. 55
Davidson, Marshall B. 66
De Gennaro, Richard 18
District of Columbia Historical Records Survey 57
Donnelly, Marian C. 40
Dunlap, Leslie W. 22

Dunlap, William 11
Dupuy, R. Ernest 71
Dupuy, Trevor N. 71

Eames, Wilberforce 16
Earle, Alice Morse 26
Eaton, Conrad P. 53
Evans, Charles 27
Evans, Luther H. 75

Farley, Richard A. 50
Fleming, Thomas 42
Flint, Austin A. 17
Ford, Gerald R. 76
Ford, Worthington Chauncey 28
Frantz, Ray W., Jr. 35
Freidel, Frank 23
Friedman, Milton 72

Gaines, Ervin J. 20
Galbraith, John Kenneth 25
Garraty, John A. 45
Garrett, Wendell 65
Gill, Brendan 43
Gill, Theodore 17
Goldstein, Kenneth S. 60
Gray, Asa 12
Gray, Lewis Cecil 50
Griffin, Grace Gardner 53

Haas, Warren J. 62
Handler, Philip 12
Handlin, Oscar 67
Harrer, Gustave A. 49
Hart, Albert Bushnell 23
Hart, James D. 70
Hay, Thomas Robson 56
Hazard, Ebenezer 3
Heyns, Roger W. 38

Historical Records Survey 57
Hoagland, H. E. 34
Hofstadter, Richard 64
Hunt, Gaillard 28
Hunt, T. Sterry 17
Hurst, John F. 17

Jaffe, Bernard 61
James, Edward T. 45
Jameson, J. Franklin 28, 42
Jensen, Oliver 66
Johnson, Allen 45
Jones, Clara S. 30

Kent, James 7
Knight, Edward H. 17
Krout, John Allen 46

Landes, David S. 33
Lawrence, Eugene 17
Leopold, Richard W. 64
Lescohier, Don D. 34
Leuchtenburg, William E. 48
Lorenz, John G. 21
Lynd, Helen Merrell 47
Lynd, Robert S. 47

McDonald, John P. 5
McElderry, Stanley 59
McMaster, John Bach 18
McNiff, Philip J. 13
Malone, Dumas 45
Matthiessen, F. O. 58
Mencken, H. L. 36
Milczewski, Marion A. 44
Miller, J. Gormly 24
Mittelman, E. B. 34
Modigliani, Franco 72
Morison, Samuel Eliot 48
Morris, Richard B. 10

Morse, Jedidiah 2
Mott, Frank Luther 54
Mumford, Lewis 40

Nebenzahl, Kenneth 16
Nevins, Allan 62
Nicholson, Thomas D. 15

Odell, George C. D. 43
O'Keeffe, Richard L. 31

Palmer, Richard E. 8
Parkman, Francis 13
Parrington, Vernon Louis 44
Paullin, Charles Oscar 49
Perlman, Selig 34
Phillips, Ulrich Bonnell 35
Potter, David Morris 69

Rhodes, James Ford 20
Rogers, Rutherford D. 9
Roosevelt, Theodore 22
Rose, Harold M. 2
Rossell, Glenora Edwards 26
Rossiter, William Sidney 31

Sabin, Joseph 16
Saposs, David J. 34
Schlesinger, Arthur Meier, Sr. 51
Schoolcraft, Henry Rowe 14
Schuyler, Robert Livingston 45
Schwartz, Anna Jacobson 72
Shank, Russell 61
Shipton, Clifford K. 27
Slosson, Edwin E. 38
Stanley, Justin A. 7
Starr, Harris E. 45
Steuermann, Clara 57
Stinehour, Roderick D. 6

Sumner, Helen L. 34
Sumner, William G. 17

Taft, Philip 34
Tarbell, Ida M. 29
Taylor, Joshua C. 11
Thacher, James 8
Thomas, Isaiah 6
Thompson, Esther Katherine 50
Thomson, Meldrim, Jr. 1
Thwaites, Reuben Gold 30
Treyz, Joseph H. 32
Tunney, Gene 46
Turner, Frederick Jackson 37
Tyler, Moses Coit 24

Vail, R. W. G. 16
Van Hise, Charles Richard 32
Veblen, Thorstein 25

Wagman, Frederick H. 14
Walker, Francis A. 17
Ward, John William 48
Ward, Robert DeCourcy 41
Warren, Charles 39
Warren, Mercy Otis 4
Wasilewski, Vincent T. 73
Webber, Jean Y. 34
Weber, David C. 56
Webster, Noah 9
Weld, Ralph Foster 56
Wells, David A. 17
Whipple, Edwin P. 17
Whitney, Virginia P. 4
Wiggins, James Russell 63
Wilson, Alexander 5
Winsor, Justin 19
Woodward, C. Vann 68
Woolsey, Theodore D. 17
Wright, John K. 49

The Stinehour Press
Lunenburg, Vermont

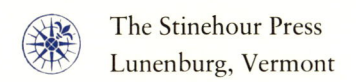

DATE DUE

ILL - Univ of NV, Reno

ILL 9-8-80